THE EVERYTHING®
BIG BOOK OF PARTY GAMES

Dear Reader,

Welcome to *The Everything® Big Book of Party Games*. As both a mother and someone who has worked for years in the party-planning business, I find myself always searching for a new game. The classics don't always work for your audience. Sometimes it's a birthday party, a family gathering, or just a rainy day. In my experience, there is always a game that will bring something more to each situation.

Years ago, I realized that just because I am an adult doesn't mean my game-playing days have to come to an end. There are times where, as an adult, you need games. Maybe it's to ease the tension in an awkward situation, to help enhance team-building skills at work, or to break the ice within an unfamiliar group. No matter your age or company, playing a game can be a strategy you use to initiate socialization. Remember how easy it was to pick up the phone when you were a kid and ask your best friend, "Want to come over and play?" It still is that easy!

I hope you enjoy the variety of games and activities in this book. Remember, there is really only one rule to playing games, and that is to have *fun*! So please let me help you do just that.

Sincerely,

Carrie Sever

Welcome to the EVERYTHING® Series!

These handy, accessible books give you all you need to tackle a difficult project, gain a new hobby, comprehend a fascinating topic, prepare for an exam, or even brush up on something you learned back in school but have since forgotten.

You can choose to read an Everything® book from cover to cover or just pick out the information you want from our four useful boxes: e-questions, e-facts, e-alerts, and e-ssentials. We give you everything you need to know on the subject, but throw in a lot of fun stuff along the way, too.

We now have more than 400 Everything® books in print, spanning such wide-ranging categories as weddings, pregnancy, cooking, music instruction, foreign language, crafts, pets, New Age, and so much more. When you're done reading them all, you can finally say you know Everything®!

PUBLISHER Karen Cooper

MANAGING EDITOR, EVERYTHING® SERIES Lisa Laing

COPY CHIEF Casey Ebert

ASSISTANT PRODUCTION EDITOR Alex Guarco

ACQUISITIONS EDITOR Pamela Wissman

DEVELOPMENT EDITOR Eileen Mullan

EVERYTHING® SERIES COVER DESIGNER Erin Alexander

Visit the entire Everything® series at *www.everything.com*

THE
EVERYTHING®
BIG BOOK OF
PARTY GAMES

Over 300 creative and fun games for all ages!

Carrie Sever

Avon, Massachusetts

An Everything® Series Book.
Everything® and everything.com® are registered trademarks of F+W Media, Inc.

Published by Adams Media, a division of F+W Media, Inc.
57 Littlefield Street, Avon, MA 02322. U.S.A.
www.adamsmedia.com

ISBN 10: 1-4405-7295-X
ISBN 13: 978-1-4405-7295-1
eISBN 10: 1-4405-7296-8
eISBN 13: 978-1-4405-7296-8

Printed in the United States of America.

10 9 8 7 6 5 4 3 2 1

Library of Congress Cataloging-in-Publication Data

Sever, Carrie.
  The everything big book of party games / Carrie Sever.
      pages cm.
  ISBN 978-1-4405-7295-1 (pb) -- ISBN 1-4405-7295-X (pb) -- ISBN 978-1-4405-7296-8 (ebook)--
ISBN 1-4405-7296-8 (ebook)
  1. Entertaining. 2. Games. 3. Parties. I. Title.
  GV1471.S46 2014
  793.2--dc23

                    2013044604

Interior illustrations by Eric Andrews.

Cover images © 123RF/Pedro Nogueira, alhovik, oleksiy, Laschon Maximilian.

This book is available at quantity discounts for bulk purchases.
For information, please call 1-800-289-0963.

Contents

Acknowledgments

I would like to thank my children, Hailey, Layla, and Layne. If it were not for their persistence of constant playtime, my knowledge of fun and games would be nonexistent. You guys are the spark in my life—thank you.

Top Ten Reasons
Everybody Loves Games

1. Everyone needs a break from the daily grind, and games are the perfect escape!

2. Games teach you to control your emotions, both when you are winning and losing.

3. They can help increase self-confidence.

4. Games help burn off some excess energy.

5. A game is a great way to get creative.

6. Everyone involved in playing will get better acquainted and connected.

7. Games encourage active participation.

8. For children, games reinforce the importance of following rules.

9. They help you brush up on your solving skills and methodical thinking.

10. A little competition never hurt anyone!

Introduction

WHO DOESN'T ENJOY PLAYING games? Whether it's a full-blown party or a casual gathering, games can become the main source of entertainment in no time flat. While many people tend to associate games with kids' birthday parties, there are so many other events and gatherings where games can be utilized to keep the attendees having fun. This book contains more than 300 fun-filled games for just about every situation, age, and purpose.

That being said, how do you choose the right game for the right situation? Aside from the classics like Pin the Tail on the Donkey, Charades, and board games, most people find themselves at a loss for new game ideas. Game selection should never be an intimidating or discouraging task. It should be fun! Being overwhelmed early in your planning can put a dent in your enthusiasm. That is why in this book you will find a large assortment of games categorized so that there is no difficulty or confusion involved.

When choosing a game, there are several things to think about. First consider the situation. Is this a child's party, and if so, how old are the children? Not all games can be comprehended or enjoyed by children of varied ages. Maybe it's an office party, and you need icebreaker games or group games based on size. Perhaps it is just a night at home with the family, and you want to keep everyone entertained. No matter the situation, this book has you covered.

The next thing to think about would be where and when the occasion will take place. Will it be outside or inside, at work or at home, at night or during the day, summer or winter? These elements are incredibly important to take into consideration. You wouldn't want to plan a game that could possibly get messy if the party is taking place in your living room, right?

When planning a gathering, there are a series of things you should do in order to pull it off without a hitch, but stressing about the party isn't one of them. The goal shouldn't be to break the bank to try to make it the most amazing party ever. The goals should be for you to not worry, to spend only what you've budgeted for the party, and to help your guests enjoy themselves. And hey, if people are talking about it for the next week, then that is a great bonus.

Before you start your exciting journey through this big book of games, just remember games are meant to be fun. They are never supposed to be overwhelming or too complicated. If they were, they wouldn't be games at all. So sit back, plan your games, and help create the moments that everyone will remember forever!

CHAPTER 1

Group Games

Incorporating games into any social situation not only helps ease the tension of meeting people for the first time and prevents the formation of cliques, it also allows everyone to get to know one another and have a blast at the same time. Likewise, with family time, sometimes kids aren't very happy to have to stop their lives and play a "boring" game. But adults and children both learn through play. The following games are far from boring and will bring any group together in laughter and learning.

Family Games

With the hustle and bustle of today's society, getting together as a family can be hard. But playing a simple game can help to reconnect everyone after a long day or week. The games don't always require a ton of preparation or supplies. In actuality, the simpler the family game, the better. The following games are fun, entertaining, and above all, simple.

The Flour Game

3 or more players

What You Need

❍ Sack of flour
❍ Butter knife or plastic knife
❍ Medium bowl
❍ Plate (with a circumference bigger than that of the bowl)
❍ Piece of candy

This game uses household items and takes some patience, but it is very fun. To start, pack the flour inside the bowl as tight as you can. Place the plate on top of the bowl, and turn it over. This will create a flour mound. Gently place the piece of candy on top of the flour mound. Each player then takes turns using the knife to slice off sections of flour without caving in the mound and losing the candy inside of it. The one who causes the mound to cave in must pick the candy out with his or her teeth. This game is indeed simple, but it can become competitive, and you will find your group wanting to play for more than just one round!

QUESTION

What if someone playing the game has a gluten allergy?
While not everyone has a severe allergy to gluten, it is always best to take precautions. With this game, you can easily switch out any flour for gluten-free flour. Another option would be to use baby powder if you would like to avoid any gluten issues.

Movie Trivia

3 or more players

What You Need

- ○ Small pieces of paper
- ○ Pencils
- ○ Bowl or container

This game gets everyone involved, even the smaller children who watch cartoons. Have everyone write down two to three popular movie or show titles on the pieces of paper (a parent can write down some ideas for the young ones). Fold them up and place the papers into a bowl or container. After mixing them up, have everyone take turns pulling a title and then acting it out. The first to successfully guess the correct movie or show title gets to go next. If no one can guess the title then the player has to go again. You can break into teams if you'd like and, when acting out, can even use a timer set at two minutes. The team that the actor is on has to guess within the time limit to earn a point. The team with the most points at the end wins.

Show-and-Tell Memory

4 or more players

What You Need

- ○ Personal items of each player

A game like this will help the family to learn a little about one another. Have players gather at least three to four items that mean something to them. Have the family get in a circle and place their items in front of them.

Starting with one item, the first player is to hold up the item and say something about it, perhaps a memory or its special meaning. He or she is to do this for each item, and once completed, place the items out of everyone's sight. The next person is to do the same. Once everyone has had a turn, place the items out of sight in a pile together.

When everyone's items are completed, the family now has to take turns pulling an item that is not theirs, naming to whom it belongs, and reciting what the memory or special meaning was. The family member with the most correct items wins the game. It can get complicated when people get very detailed about their items. Having to remember after seeing so many items and hearing so many stories can confuse anyone. It's a game of memory strength and paying attention.

FACT

According to Familyfacts.org, a family that spends time together doing some type of activity will experience greater bonding as a family unit. The children in these families tend to have a better academic performance as well.

Storytelling Chain

3 or more players

Storytelling helps everyone to use his or her imagination. This game invites children of many ages to play right alongside the adults. Have everyone sit in a circle and the oldest person start the story with a classic line like, "Once upon a time," or "There once was a prince/princess." The person will continue the story for a couple of lines and then the next person will take over, who can take the story in any direction he or she likes. This game aids children in expressing their fears, wants, and creativity. In addition, there is nothing quite like hearing your children giggle over building a tale with the family.

Youth Group Games

Youth groups help young people form friendships with their peers. These groups also aid in encouraging young people and building confidence. Youth groups often utilize games to accomplish these goals. Most games are centered on teamwork and growing as a group.

Caterpillar Race

8 or more players (at least 2 groups of 4)

What You Need

❍ A bed sheet for each group

This game can be played indoors or outdoors depending on the weather or environment. Begin by having the youth group split into several teams, dividing as evenly as possible. Then have each team split in half and stand across the room from each other. Pick a side and hand a bed sheet to the first players on each team.

The mission is for them to lie down and wrap themselves in the bed sheet by rolling around in it. Once they are covered, they must caterpillar-crawl on their bellies across to the other side where the other half of their team is waiting. They must then unroll from the sheet for the next players to use. This continues until everyone has had a turn. The fastest team to complete the race wins.

ABC Roundup

10 or more players (at least 2 groups of 5)

A group game like this has the teams work together to reach a collective goal. Each team will empty their pockets, purses, and book bags to try and get as many items as they can that start with a letter in the alphabet. For example, lip balm, mirror, and wallet would work for the letters L, M, and W. The team to collect the most letters of the alphabet wins. You can choose to let the players allow brand names as acceptable points, but only one letter can be used per item.

Asking the Leader

6 or more players

What You Need

○ Sticky notes
○ Pens of the same color
○ A large cube or die to roll with

This is a great question-and-answer game. Have the players write down questions on sticky notes; they can write down as many as they like, just make sure there is only one to a note. Have the leader go around and collect the questions. Using the large cube or die, place a question on each side and have a youth member roll it on the floor or a table. Once it settles, he or she will read off the question and give his or her view on the subject.

The leader will then give his or her opinion on the subject. Once this is completed, the next youth member will roll. This will continue until all questions have been asked. Feel free to let the youth group discuss the issues at hand. Use this as an opportunity to build communication within and provoke thoughts on things they may have never considered.

ESSENTIAL

Youth groups gather to help one another bond and discuss current issues. Sometimes the issues or questions can be embarrassing or may be something that kids just don't feel comfortable discussing openly. A game like Asking the Leader helps address these issues without exposing the questioner.

Back to Back

Large group of players

Have two players sit on the floor, back to back. The object is to try to stand up without the use of your hands. It is definitely harder than it seems and requires everyone to work to stand together. With each successful stand up, add another player. Continue until they can no longer stand as a whole. This is a great team-building game to get the youth working as a unit.

Character-Building Games

Character is very similar to the definition of personality. It is the way someone thinks, feels, and behaves, and everyone's character is unique. The importance of character is seen in how people deal with each other and the situations that are thrown their way. Helping one another to build character can be done easily through playing games. This can happen without the participants even realizing that the game itself is helping them. The following games are perfect for building one's character.

Compliments All Around

Medium-to-large group of players

This game focuses on respect and works for almost any age that can understand the concept of a compliment. Have the group mingle for ten minutes, asking one another simple questions about themselves. Once the ten minutes is up, have everyone stand in a circle. The person who starts is to look at the person on his or her left and compliment that person in some way. This will continue around the circle until it is back to the beginning. At this point, they will reverse and go to the right. This gives everyone a great boost of confidence and helps others to realize it never hurts to encourage your peers.

The Identity Game

5 or more players

What You Need

○ Scraps of paper
○ Pens
○ Plastic bag

Another important character trait is self-worth. In this activity, the participants will have a chance to boost their confidence. Have the players grab a pen and paper and write down five things about themselves that make them who they are—the things they are proud of, such as being good at a sport, helping clean the house, or how they love animals. Once they are done, have them fold the papers in half and place them in the plastic bag.

The leader will then pick a paper and read it aloud without saying to whom it belongs. The group or has to then guess who they think the list is about and must supply a reason they think it is that person. This can be done either as a group or by having everyone take a guess. By the end of the game, everyone will feel good about him- or herself, and others will have learned something about their fellow players.

FACT

According to the *Merriam-Webster Dictionary*, the definition of *character* is "the complex of mental and ethical traits marking and often individualizing a person, group, or nation." Essentially, *character* makes up who we are and what we stand for.

The Walk

2 or more groups of players

What You Need

❍ Several boards (at least 8 is good)

Played outdoors, this activity builds responsibility, trust, and decision-making skills. You will need to gather several wooden boards. Old lumber works well—just make sure there are no nails, staples, screws, splinters, etc. in them. The size of the boards be can whatever you like, but you want to make sure they are long enough so that the players can walk on them.

Place the boards flat on the ground to make two or more winding paths, one for each team. Leave about a foot between each board. Have the participants split into groups, and choose a leader for each group. The objective of the game is for the team leaders to guide their team from one end of the path to the other.

What's the catch? The team walking the boards must hold hands while keeping their eyes closed, with only the first and last person in the chain allowed to have their eyes open, and no one can step off the boards. If someone steps off, the entire team must start over. The team members can guide each other with communication, such as planning their route or strategy before starting, talking each other through it, or trusting the person in front of them. The team to finish with the best time wins.

Reunion Games

Reunions can range anywhere from family and school to bands and military affiliation. Getting together with people from the past can be a bit overwhelming for some, but the focus should be to enjoy reliving great memories and learning who the people you once knew have become.

Secrets

Medium to large group

What You Need

❍ Paper
❍ Pen
❍ Container to hold papers

Everyone that wants to participate in this game will write his or her name down on a piece of paper and place it in the container. Once everyone has finished this, have each player draw a name and keep it a secret. Throughout the reunion, players are to ask these people questions about themselves—as random as they choose. They must do this without letting them know they have picked them and without telling anyone what was discussed.

Once the reunion is winding down, have all the players gather back together. One by one, they will stand up and say, "I know a secret and it is . . . ," which is followed by revealing the secret but not the person it pertains to. Everyone now has to guess who it is about. The person to guess the most correct wins the game.

Hot Phototato!

What You Need

❍ Camera with auto-flash capability
❍ Props like goofy hats, scarves, glasses, etc.

Reunions are the perfect time for tons of picture taking. This game makes it so you aren't running around having to snap photos while trying to enjoy the reunion itself. Have everyone gather in a group and use the props you have supplied. Set the auto flash on the camera and then have everyone pass the camera around, holding and posing for a second, then passing the camera on. It will take a lot of photos, so everyone will have a chance to photo-bomb each other with funny faces and gestures. Once you are done, you can gather e-mail addresses and offer to e-mail the photos later.

ALERT

How's Yours?

Guessing games are always fun, and this guessing game is great at any reunion. Have the people willing to play the game gather in a group and select one person to be the "odd man out." This person will step out of the room or away from hearing distance of the group. Pick an item everybody has in common, like a car. When the odd man out is asked back, everyone is to say one word that applies to the chosen item.

For a car, people could say the color, the year, that it's fast or that it's dirty, or anything to describe it in one word. The odd man out has to try to guess what it is they are talking about, and this usually prompts hilarious answers. When the person has guessed the selected item or has given up, a new odd man out can be chosen.

Outdoor Group Games

Playing outdoors opens up a whole new type of game play. Things can get a little messy and/or involve a lot of exercise and movement. The group sizes may range in numbers, but the level of fun should still be great. These outdoor games are exciting and good for a laugh.

Electricity

Two medium-to-large groups of players, with the same number of players on each team

What You Need

○ Coin for flipping
○ Ball (basketball-size for easy grasp)

Begin this game by asking for a volunteer to be the "shot caller" and then divide the players into two teams, with the same number of players on each team. Have the teams line up and stand facing each other. Place the ball at the end of the line, at an even distance between both teams. Have the teams hold hands with one another. The shot caller will flip the coin and announce heads or tails. When it is heads, the first person will squeeze the hand of the next person, who will squeeze the hand of the next person, and continue until the last hand is squeezed. If it is tails, the shot caller flips until the coin comes up heads.

Of course, this game is based on the idea that everyone will be honest about his hand being squeezed before pursuing the ball. The anticipation that builds when playing this game should have everyone amped by the time it's his turn to get the ball. The last person must then run over and try to get the ball before the other team does. For each time the ball is gathered, that team receives a point. After each turn, the last person will go to the front of the line and it will start again. Once there is a full rotation, the team with the most points wins.

Down to the Ground

Small-to-large group of players

What You Need

○ Tennis Ball

This game doesn't require much athletic skill, but players must be able to at least toss a ball. Have everyone in the group spread out from one another in a circle, and hand someone the tennis ball. The person with the ball will underhand-throw the ball to anyone he or she chooses. If the person catches it, that player then throws it to someone else. If the ball is dropped, that player must get down on one knee, then toss the ball to the next person.

Everyone continues to toss the ball around, but each time a player drops the ball, he or she must get further down, starting with one knee, then both knees, followed by one elbow, then both elbows, and lastly the chin to the ground. Players can continue to catch and toss the ball with chins to the ground, but they will be out with the next catch they miss. Last player standing wins the game.

ALERT

For any game that involves a lot of movement, it's best to have everyone stretch a bit before playing. This is a great way to avoid any injuries while getting everyone loosened up and ready to go!

Your Land, My Land

2 medium-to-large groups of players

What You Need

❍ Rope, hose, or spray paint to create a separator
❍ Beanbags, colored plastic balls, or anything cheap and in abundance
❍ Timer or watch

This is a great way to get a little competition going when there is a group involved. Separate the participants into two separate groups. Split the playing area into two distinct "lands" using a rope or a hose, or by spray painting a line on the grass. Toss the beanbags, or whatever items you chose, so they are spread out evenly over both sides. The mission is to get the most items on your land in twenty minutes.

You cannot move the items that are on your side, so you must enter the other land to get the items to your side. But beware: Once both of your feet are on the other side, you can be tagged and must sit down until someone from your team comes to rescue you by tagging you. Once time is up, the team with the most items on their side wins.

Indoor Group Games

When playing indoors, you have to consider the size of area you have to work with. You also must think about keeping the group safe, involved, and happy. Playing indoors can be just as fun as outdoors; it just takes the right game to make it happen.

Improv in a Bag

3 or more small-to-large groups of players

What You Need

○ A bag for each team
○ Random items from around the house

It's time to brush up on your creativity and improvisation skills! This game challenges players to use their acting skills as well as teamwork. Divide players into teams, and give each team a bag of random household items as props to create a skit. Each team has ten minutes to come up with the best skit they can by using every item in the bag. The catch is that the players cannot use the items for what their actual purpose is.

For example, if you are given a spoon, you can't use it to insinuate eating, but you could use it as a drumstick to pretend playing the drums. Once time is up, each team must perform their skit in front of the rest of the group. Performing is fun in and of itself, but you can also make this a point-based game by giving each household item a point value depending on the difficulty to use it, and the team who has the most points at the end wins. If there is a tie in the end, then the teams will have to perform one last skit and the other teams will vote on whose was the best.

QUESTION

What if the game isn't being played in a home?
Wherever the game is being played, you can gather items from people's cars, the building you are in, or simply from one another. As long as you come up with enough items to play the game, you can make it work!

Fishbowl

Medium-to-large group of players

What You Need

❍ Pen
❍ Paper
❍ Bowl
❍ Scraps of paper
❍ Timer

This is a three-round game that several teams can play. There is very little preparation involved in this game. On each scrap of paper, write the name of a character or person that everyone will most likely know. Fold up each scrap and place it in the bowl.

Once all the players are in a room together, separate them into teams. One person from a team will stand up, pull a paper out of the bowl, and read the name to himself and not let anyone know what it says. That person now has one minute to verbally and/or physically describe the character without saying the name. If that person's team guesses correctly before the timer goes off, they can continue pulling names and acting them out until time is up. They receive a point for each name guessed.

Then the next team will pick a person to do the same and continue until their time is up. Once all the names are emptied from the bowl, the teams will start the next round. In round two, the major rule is to not say a word, only use actions to describe the character. Round three's rule is that only one word can be used to describe the character. The team with the most points at the end of the three rounds wins the game.

Cups and Downs

2 small-to-medium groups of players

What You Need

○ Plastic cups (two separate colors)
○ Timer

Have players separate into two teams and assign the teams a color of cups. One team will be the Ups and one team will be the Downs. Place around forty cups in the middle of the room, half of them facing up and half of them facing down. Have the Ups team stand in front of the cups facing down and have the Downs team stand in front of the cups facing up. Set the timer for one minute, and notify the teams that they have one minute to flip the cups to face the opposite direction. The team that has the most cups flipped at the end of the timer wins.

CHAPTER 2

Age-Appropriate Party Games

Not all games are appropriate for every age. Sometimes knowing which game is right for the age group you have is the hardest part of party planning. It doesn't have to be so complicated! Here are some games that are categorized by age group to make things as easy as possible.

Preschoolers (Ages 3–5)

Preschoolers can be a restless bunch, just overflowing with intense energy most people only wish they could have. Getting the little ones to sit still or wind down can be a daunting task; however, playing a game can get preschoolers to focus and tire themselves out without even noticing what's going on. Try these games and take a break from the game of constant keep up.

Pass the Parcel

5 or more players

What You Need

❍ Pieces of candy
❍ Wrapping paper or newspaper
❍ Small prize

Most preschoolers get excited over unwrapping gifts, whether it is theirs or not. The suspense and curiosity about what is inside drives them to tear through the paper. This game allows every child to unwrap a small gift, layer by layer, so that he or she can get excited about what is inside. In preparing for this game, you will need to pick a small prize that is simple to wrap.

Within each layer of wrapping paper, place a piece of candy in the wrapping. The best way to do it is to have at least twice the layers of how many children are attending. That way they receive at least two pieces of candy each during the game play. The child who reaches the last layer of wrapping paper wins the prize inside.

Clothespin Drop

3 or more players

What You Need

❍ Chair

❍ Large-mouth jar
❍ Clothespins

This is a game that will allow the children to have friendly competition without anyone feeling left out or lost. Place a jar by the back legs of a chair. Have a child, depending on height, stand or kneel on the chair facing the back. Hand them five clothespins and let each child take turns trying to drop the pins into the jar. The child who drops the most in wins a prize. With kids who are preschool age, it's sometimes best to reward each child with something small and then give the winner a little extra prize.

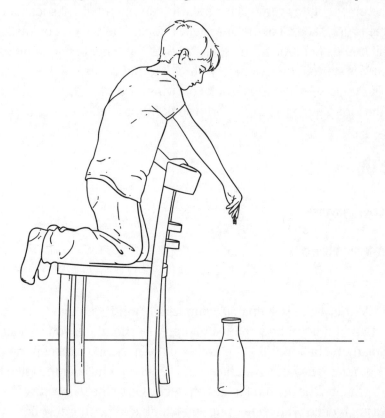

ALERT

To avoid any accidents during Clothespin Drop, you may want to have someone stand at the back of the chair and maybe even put a foot on the seat to avoid tipping. Also, warn the children not to lean on the chair while dropping the pins.

Box o' Socks

3 or more players

What You Need

- ○ Empty box or laundry basket
- ○ Tons of socks
- ○ Timer

The object of this game is to see who can put the most socks on before the time is up. Place all of the unmatched socks into the box or basket. Have the children gather around the socks and set the timer to two minutes. Once the timer is started, the children will race to put on as many socks as they can. The child with the most socks on wins. You can do several rounds to keep the kids giggling. Using colorful socks adds a little pizzazz to the game.

Keep It Up

4 or more players

What You Need

- ○ Air-filled balloons

While this game is simple, it is amazingly fun for all ages and very easy to do. Depending on how many children are attending, you can start with more than one balloon. Tell the children the mission is to keep the balloon off the ground. They can use their hands, feet, or whatever they like to keep it up. Toss it into the air and let the fun begin. Once the game is over, you can reward each child with something small for his or her hard work.

Kids (Ages 6–9)

Kids (ages 6–9) are a bit easier to entertain, since they have a better level of understanding for rules and boundaries. This age group tends to be the least picky when it comes to playing games. They are happy just getting to interact with others their age. Here are some games to get them started.

Pop and Stop

3 or more players

What You Need

❍ Bubbles

This game will get a laugh from any child by the time it's over. Have the children stand so they're spread out from one another, either inside or outside. The rules of this game state that when a bubble is blown, the children must begin laughing and moving around.

When the bubble pops, they have to stop making noise and freeze where they stand. The last to stop moving and laughing is out and must go sit on the side. The children who are out can attempt to make the other children laugh to get them out as well. The last child still in the game wins.

FACT

You can make your own bubbles at home by mixing one cup of water, two tablespoons of corn syrup, and four tablespoons of liquid dish soap. You can even use it as an opportunity to show everyone how to do it at home.

Blind Man's Bluff

6 or more players

What You Need

❍ Blindfold

Though this is considered a classic game, it is a game most people have forgotten about. Ask for a volunteer to be "It" on the first round. Place a blindfold on the child and then have the other children spread out until the person who is "It" says to freeze. Now the person who is "It" will scour the room searching for people while saying "blind man's," and everyone else must say "bluff." Hearing the "bluff" after saying "blind man's" will help the child who is "It" to find people. Once everyone has been found, the game starts over with a new person becoming "It."

FACT

According to the *Encyclopedia Britannica*, Blind Man's Bluff was played more than 2,000 years ago in ancient Greece. It is known all over the world by a variety of different names, but has continued to be played and passed down as a beloved children's game.

Smell It, Hear It

3 or more players

What You Need

- ❍ Small containers
- ❍ Paper
- ❍ Glue or tape
- ❍ Household items (spices, paperclips, fruits, buttons, etc.)

This game is all about helping children sharpen their senses. Cover the outside of each container with paper so that the kids can't see what's inside, and then number each container. For the items that have to be guessed by hearing them, make sure the lids are on tight, since they will most likely be shaken around.

For the items to smell, you can open them and let them sniff them or choose to pass them around. Give each child paper and a pen, and as the containers are passed around, the children will use their senses to try and figure out the contents. Have them write down their guesses, and at the end of the game, the child with the most correct guesses wins the game.

Make Me Laugh

4 or more players

What You Need

❍ Chair

Laughing is the best medicine for almost anything, and this game surely brings the giggles to the table. Start by placing a chair in the middle of the room. Now have all the kids stand in a circle around the chair and ask a volunteer to sit in the chair. The person in the chair has to keep a straight face as long as he or she can.

In the meantime, everyone else is taking turns to try to make that person laugh. Each time they make someone laugh they get a point. Once the person in the chair laughs, someone else will take that person's place. The person with the most points at the end of the game wins.

Tweens (Ages 10–12)

Tweens are a little harder to entertain than younger children. They are stepping out of the pretend-play with dolls and toys and venturing into more of a teenage realm. Though they are not quite there, most of them like to act as if they are. Why not cater to their imagination the best you can with these games?

Commercial Game

4 or more players

What You Need

❍ Random household items

Tweens tend to love drama and any chance to act something out. This game will give them their chance to do so. Have someone volunteer to be first in the game, and have him or her stand while everyone else is seated. Someone from the group will choose a random item from around the house and hand it to the person standing. That person will then have two minutes to come up with a commercial for that item. Then he or she has to act out a thirty-second commercial about the product. The one with the most creativity wins the game.

Candy Relay

4 or more players

What You Need

- ○ Candies such as Skittles or M&Ms
- ○ Plastic cups
- ○ Drinking straws without the bend in them
- ○ Large bowl for candy

This is a sweet little game that uses a yummy treat as part of the fun. Place a cup and straw in front of each participant. Pour the candy in the bowl and place the bowl on the other side of the room on a table. The object of the game is for participants to use the straw to suck up a piece of candy and keep it on the straw long enough to bring it across the room to their cup and drop it in. The person with the most candies in his or her cup at the end wins the game.

ESSENTIAL

After you have played Candy Relay, you can use the leftover candy as fillers for grab bags or party favors. That way, the candy doesn't go to waste, and it takes care of giving a little something special to your guests for attending your party.

Ball Battle

6 or more players

What You Need

- ❍ 2 large kitchen spoons
- ❍ 2 tennis balls

A little friendly competition is always a good thing. This game is played one on one. Each person will receive a spoon and a ball. Players are to place the ball on the spoon, and the object of the game is to keep the ball on the spoon while attempting to knock your opponents' balls off of their spoons. All the players will be scrambling to keep their ball and spoon safe. The last person with the ball still on his or her spoon wins the game.

Back-to-Back Sumo

6 or more players

What You Need

- ❍ Sheets of newspaper

Sumo wrestling can be quite entertaining to watch, so why not bring it to the party? With variations of course, this game can make for good laughs. Place a sheet of newspaper, spread out, on the ground. Two people, the sumo wrestlers, will stand back-to-back, shoulders touching, on top of the newspaper. They now have to try to push each other off the newspaper.

The first person to step off is out and someone new comes in to try. The person who wins the round gets a point each time. This continues until everyone has tried. The sumo with the most points at the end wins the game.

Teens (Ages 13–19)

Teens may want to be treated as adults, but playing a game can still be ultimately fun for them. It helps to keep them connected to their peers and to realize their age and enjoy it while it lasts.

Tag 'em and Bag 'em

8 or more players

What You Need

- ○ Clothespins
- ○ Paper
- ○ Pen
- ○ Pillowcase

This game requires a bit of preparation, but it is well worth it to get the laughs going. To start you will need to write down several different challenges for people to do. You could write something like "Dance like a chicken," "Tell everyone a secret about yourself," and "Say the alphabet backwards." Place all the papers in the pillowcase. As the players arrive, hand each one a couple of clothespins.

The object of the game is to try to pin someone without the person knowing, so, for example, clipping a clothespin on the back of someone's shirt. Once someone has been pinned, the pinner walks away and yells, "Tag 'em and bag 'em!" Everyone now has to count down from five while all players search for who got pinned. If they don't find the pin in time, then they have to pull from the bag and do whatever is on the paper. If they do find it in time, the game continues on with the next person getting pinned.

Puff Ball Fight

6 or more players

What You Need

○ Pantyhose
○ Flour
○ Paper and pen for keeping score

It doesn't have to be cold or snowing outside to have a snowball fight, but you will probably want to play this one outside to avoid things getting too messy. With these snowless puff balls you can start the fight any day of the week. To prepare the puff balls, you will need to fill the foot part of the panty hose with about a half cup of flour, cut an inch above the flour, pull tight, and tie off.

Continue filling the pantyhose up, making sure to tie off one end before putting in the flour, and follow up with tying it off to contain the flour. You should get around five snowballs per leg. Since these puff balls do not bust right away, giving everyone two or three each works just fine.

You can choose to set up teams or to play the game as individual players. However you opt to play, design your scoreboard after that. Each time a player makes contact with another player using the puffballs, he or she will receive a point. The player or team with the most points at the end wins.

Cucumber Pass

6 or more players

What You Need

○ Cucumber

This is a great game to incorporate teamwork with the teens. Have everyone stand in a circle, and have one person put the cucumber between his or her knees. That person now has to pass the cucumber to the next person without dropping it. If the person giving or receiving drops the cucumber, then he or she is out of the game. The last two to make it to the end are the winners of the game.

QUESTION

Do you have to use a cucumber, or food in general, to play Cucumber Pass?
You can use any object that has a similar weight and shape to a cucumber. Any item can be used that you can pass between the knees with little complication and no mess.

Gum Bobbing

3 or more players

What You Need

- ○ Paper plates
- ○ Whipped cream
- ○ Bubble gum

Bobbing for apples is a classic game, but why not put a twist on it? It's best to prepare this one when none of the players are in the room—that way they don't know where on the plate you have placed the gum. Put a piece of unwrapped gum on each plate and cover the gum and plate in whipped cream. The object of the game is to retrieve the gum without using your hands, chew it, and blow a bubble before anyone else does. The first one to blow the bubble wins the game.

Young Adults (Ages 20–30)

Playing games is just as important for adults as it is for children. It keeps everyone involved, continuously learning, and having fun. It gets harder to find time to cut loose the older you get, so use these games to relax and laugh!

The Fame Game

8 or more players

As the guests arrive at your party, inform them that they are to pick a famous person to act like for the rest of the night. They cannot tell anyone who they are, but they can give clues as the night goes on. By the end of the night, the people who think they know who someone was pretending to be can take a guess. The ones who guess the most correct will win the game.

Freeze Out

6 or more players

Sometimes the simplest of games can be the most fun. To set up this game, start by assigning or taking a volunteer to be Mr. or Mrs. Freeze. As the gathering goes on, Mr. or Mrs. Freeze will randomly freeze completely still until people start to notice and freeze as well. The last one to freeze has to be Mr. or Mrs. Freeze from that point on. The ones who never become Mr. or Mrs. Freeze are the winners.

ESSENTIAL

A good variation on Freeze Out is to give the person playing the part of Mr. or Mrs. Freeze a foam finger, hat, or bow tie. Upon freezing, he or she will put on the item to help others notice that it's time to follow suit!

Take a Hike!

8 or more players

What You Need

○ Enough chairs for all but one guest

It's time to have some fun and get to know one another at the same time! Put all the chairs in a circle and have one person stand in the center. Have all the other participants take a seat in a chair. The person in the middle now makes a statement, only one at a time, about his or her likes or dislikes, qualities, or life experiences.

For example, the person could say, "If you don't like coconut, take a hike"; "If you have ever been to New York, take a hike"; or "If you have ever run a marathon, take a hike." Whomever this applies to, along with the middleman, has to get up and find new seats. The one to not find a seat now has to be in the middle and make a statement. This game can go on as long as you like because it's always good for a laugh.

Pick Up

8 or more players

Offering a prize will usually get the people who aren't too crazy about participating to be the first to want to play. This game offers a prize, but you have to work to get it. Have all your guests gather around in a circle and link elbows. Place a prize in the center, such as money or another popular item—something that will really get the players to compete. When a nonplayer yells "Go," the players will try to get the prize. They can try to keep each other back by pulling or resisting, but they cannot break the chain. The person to get the prize gets to keep it. Feel free to do more than one round. I'm sure your guests wouldn't mind at all.

Adults (Ages 30 and Up)

There's no better way to liven up a party than to introduce a game. If not all your guests are willing to play, don't worry about it. They'll join in eventually when they see how much fun everyone else is having!

Two Truths and a Lie

6 or more players

This is a good way to see just how well you and your guests know one another. Have your guests gather around and think up two truths and one lie about themselves. They are not to tell one another anything, just keep it to themselves. Advise them that it's best to pick something small and believable as the lie and the truths to be something more extreme if possible. One at a time, they will reveal two truths and a lie to the group. It is now up to the group to figure out what the lie is.

No, No, No

8 or more players

What You Need

❍ Leis or beaded necklaces

This is a game that takes little effort other than attention and listening skills. As the guests arrive, hand them one lei/necklace each. During the gathering, they are forbidden from saying the word *no*. If someone hears them say *no*, that person gets to take his or her lei/necklace. If a person has more than one lei/necklace and slips up and says *no*, he or she only loses one lei/necklace at a time. The person who has the most leis/necklaces at the end wins.

FACT

"What do most Nobel laureates, innovative entrepreneurs, artists and performers, well-adjusted children, happy couples and families, and the most successfully adapted mammals have in common? They play enthusiastically throughout their lives."—Stuart Brown, National Institute for Play

Gargle a Tune

4 or more players

What You Need

○ Glasses of water for your guests

There are a couple of options for setting up for this game. You can write down a bunch of songs on pieces of paper or you can let your guests choose their own songs, but the catch is that they have to put water in their mouth and gargle the tune until someone can guess just what it is. The person with the most correct guesses wins the game. A gracious host will keep a bucket nearby for guests post-gargle!

Bite the Bag

3 or more players

What You Need

○ Paper grocery-size bag

Most of the time, when you search for an adult game, the games are either based on drinking or the supplies that are needed are overwhelming. This game only needs one item and doesn't involve drinking of any sort. All you need to do is place an opened paper bag on the floor. Have participants stand in front of the bag one at a time. They must pick up the bag with their mouth while their hands are behind their back.

Sounds mighty simple at first, but for each time the bag is picked up, players must fold the top of the bag over one time. As it gets further down, it gets a little more complicated. Also, the only parts of the body that can touch the ground are the feet. The person to go the lowest is the winner of this game.

CHAPTER 3

Competition Games

A little friendly competition is always a good idea. Not only does it keep the adrenaline flowing, testing your abilities and sometimes your problem-solving skills, but it can help keep you sharp and feeling confident. Whether competing as a team or as an individual, you should focus on having fun and not on whether you're winning or losing. So bring the competition to your next event with the games in this section.

Family-Friendly Competition Games

Since families come in all sizes and ages, the games they play need to have variety as well. The games should involve everyone so that all members feel they are part of the whole scheme of play. The following games are competitive, but just enough to allow a winner and still create good memories.

Toss and Catch

6 or more players

What You Need

- ❍ Plastic bowl
- ❍ Ribbon or string
- ❍ Small beanbags or any small, soft items for tossing

There is some preparation for this game, but it is minimal. You will need to punch a hole on each side of the bowl and run the ribbon through it. This bowl will be tied on top of every player's head at one point or another, so leave extra ribbon to adjust accordingly. Separate the players into teams of two. One will wear the bowl/hat and the other will be the one tossing. Have the one tossing stand at least five feet from the one with the bowl on his or her head. With one minute on the clock, the teams will have to toss as many beanbags as they can into the bowl. The team with the most bags in their hat at the end of the game wins.

FACT

According to the American Heart Association, one in three children or adolescents is overweight or obese. Much of it has to do with being inactive while watching television or playing with electronic devices. This is a great reason to initiate active play as a family. It's good for your health and happiness!

Horse

3 or more players

What You Need

○ Basketball
○ Basketball hoop or large empty trashcan

Getting outside and exercising as a family is a wonderful way to practice healthy living. Shooting baskets has never been so fun than with a game of Horse. In this game, the players will take turns shooting the ball, trying to make a basket. The first player that makes a basket gets an "H." Every time that person makes a basket after that, another letter is gained until *Horse* is spelled.

The catch is that wherever the basket is made from or how it is made originally, the following players must do the same to get their letter. If no one has made a basket for a full round, then people can choose where they want to stand and how they will throw their ball to try to make it harder for everyone else to complete. The first to spell *Horse* wins the game.

ESSENTIAL

The game of Horse does not require having a basketball hoop at home. You can play at a gym or other facility that has a basketball court. You can even use a large trashcan to play with if there is no hoop available. Get creative!

Rhyme Time

3 or more players

Family conversations can be repetitive with, "How was your day?" "What happened in school?" and "What do you want for dinner?" This game will give you a way to keep a conversation going without the same old questions. The object of the game is simple—just use rhymes to complete the sentence.

The game may start off with a pace that seems slow, but as it continues, your rhyming talents will show. The subjects will change and laughter you'll hear, so please enjoy the game because fun is near (see how fun?).

Apple on a String

3 or more players, ages 8 and up

What You Need

○ Apple
○ Board with nail hammered through
○ String

This game is a bit harder than most people think it is at first. Place the board up against a tree or wall, secured so it will not fall, with the nail pointed outward. Tie the string around the apple to secure it, with enough string left over that you are able to swing it. Each person will line up to swing the apple at the board, trying to get the apple to hit the nail and stay put. Each player gets three tries, and then it is the next person's turn. You can do rounds and give points for success or just play to have fun.

ALERT

Apple on a String is better suited for children ages 8 or older because there is an exposed nail involved. To avoid injuries, make sure the players stand back from the board at a safe distance, and that the board is secured at all times. Also, be sure to get rid of the board after the game is over, to avoid any injuries later on.

Kid-Friendly Competition Games

Kids love to play games that name a winner. Feeling like they have accomplished something is very rewarding for children. The important part is to make sure to explain that winning is fine, but gloating is not permitted.

Playing competitive games should supply the kids with a good competition experience and tons of fun.

Handful o' Beans

6 or more players

What You Need

❍ 2 large bags of dried beans
❍ A bucket or bowl for each team

If you can hold on to a handful of beans while you do a simple somersault, then you can play this game. Have the kids separate into two teams and line up one behind the other. Place a bucket on the other side of the play area in front of each team, and put a bag full of beans next to the first person in each line.

When the game begins, the first person in line from each team will grab a handful of beans and begin somersaulting to the side with the buckets. When they arrive, they must put the beans in their bucket and run back to tag the hand of another teammate. The teammate does the same as the first person. This continues until everyone has gone through at least once; you can do it twice if the teams are small. The team with the highest bean count wins the game.

Double Egg Relay

4 or more players

What You Need

❍ 2 whole uncooked eggs for each player

This game is very much like trying to pat your head and rub your belly at the same time—it's very possible to do, but it requires concentration. To start this game, you will need to create a start line and a finish line that are about twenty feet apart from each other.

Players will place an egg under their chin and hold it to their neck. They will then put an egg on the ground in front of them. At the start of the game, they have to push the egg to the finish line using their feet or hands while they keep the other egg under their chin and keep from dropping it.

The first person to cross the finish line with both eggs not broken wins the game. If no one completes the game with two eggs intact, the winner is the first person to cross with one egg unbroken.

ALERT

Before playing Double Egg Relay, it is always best to talk with the parents first about whether their kids have allergies. Some children have egg allergies, and some are more severe than others. Asking parents beforehand can avoid any health issues.

Shoe Hunt

6 or more players

What You Need

○ Shoes, shoes, shoes

As your guests arrive, have them take off their shoes. Using the guests' shoes and any extra shoes you have around the house, create a pile in the middle of a room. Make sure to mix up the shoes as much as possible. Once you are ready to begin the game, have all the players come in with their eyes closed. On the count of three, they can open their eyes and begin to dig through the pile to find their shoes. They can move the shoes around as much as they like to keep the other players from finding their own shoes. The player to find his or her shoes first wins the game.

Teen Competition Games

Most teens are all about proving that they have what it takes to be winners. The following games provide teens with an opportunity to do just that. And all the while they will be learning, laughing, and interacting with one another.

Cheesy Cap

4 or more players

What You Need

- ○ Shower caps
- ○ Shaving cream
- ○ Timer
- ○ Cheese puffs

This game will give everyone a good chuckle or two. Split the teens into pairs of teams and set the timer at one minute. One team member will wear a shower cap covered in shaving cream and the other will toss cheese puffs onto the shower cap. However, the one tossing the cheese puffs must spin in a circle two times before beginning to toss. The team with the most puffs on their heads after the time is up wins.

Stuffed

2 teams of 4 or more

What You Need

○ 2 extra-large or larger T-shirts, the bigger the better, 1 for each team
○ Balloons (9" are usually the best to use)
○ Stopwatch

Have the smallest person on each team put the T-shirt on and tuck it into his or her pants. Set the stopwatch for ninety seconds. Once the game starts, the remaining team members will have to blow up the balloons and stuff them into the shirt as fast as they can. When time is up, the team with the most balloons in their shirts wins the game.

ALERT

When playing Stuffed, ask the participants if they are allergic to latex. Latex allergies can be life threatening, so if you know that someone is allergic, you might want to rethink this game, or any others involving balloons, and try another one that doesn't involve any latex.

Musical Balance

5 or more players

What You Need

○ Background music
○ A book for each player

This is just like musical chairs, but with an awesome twist. Prepare some music to play in the background during the game. Hand the players a book each, and tell them they will need to balance it on their head. When the music starts they will walk around the room, keeping the book balanced. When the music stops, all the players must stop and kneel down on one knee. If their book drops they are out. Once the music starts again, they have to stand back up and continue to walk the room until the music stops again. The last person with the book still balanced on his or her head wins the game.

Memory Games

The older you get and the more information you accumulate, the harder it is to remember everything. On an average day, a lot of information passes through the human brain without being absorbed. Here are some games to help develop a better memory through the use of play.

Going on a Picnic

4 or more players

Players pretend they are going on a picnic. They begin by saying, "I'm going on a picnic and I'm bringing . . . " People have to say what the person/persons before them said plus what they are bringing. If they skip an item or can't remember, they are out. Last person to recite the list correctly wins. An alternate way to play is to use the alphabet. Each turn will require that item to begin with the next letter in the alphabet.

Where Was It?

5 or more players

What You Need

❍ Tray
❍ Random items

Have the players gather around. Bring out a tray with several items on it. Let the first player look at it for one minute and then turn around and take everything off the tray. The player must then try to put the items back where they were on the tray from memory. If that player gets it right, you add an item. The same player continues until he or she can no longer remember what the arrangement was and then you move on to the next player. The person to remember the most correct wins.

FACT

People who have amazingly detailed and unfathomable memories are known as *mnemonists*. Russian journalist Solomon Shereshevskii had a rare ability for memory and data recall. He could recite entire speeches, extremely long lists, and complicated math formulas after hearing them only one time.

Name the Difference

6 or more players

This will definitely test people's memory and attentiveness. Start by having two people enter the room. Everyone playing the game must observe them. They then leave the room and either switch, remove, or alter something about themselves. When they return to the room, the players must name what the differences are. The player with the most accurate observation wins.

Team Trivia Games

Working as a team toward a common goal is fun. Competing as a team against another team is even more fun. The following games give everyone the chance to be a winner.

Guess That Tune

5 or more players

What You Need

○ Container or bowl

❍ Paper
❍ Pen

Trivia is meant to test how much knowledge you have about a certain category. This game is going to test how familiar your guests are with past and current music. The catch is that the players themselves have to hum the tune.

Before your trivia guests arrive, you will need to write down popular songs from the past and ones that are currently popular. Place the papers in the container and mix them up. Have your guests pull a paper and hum the tune until someone can guess what it is. For every correct guess, players receive one point. The player with the most points at the end wins the game.

Name the Celebrity

4 or more players

What You Need

❍ Old magazines
❍ Scissors
❍ Glue
❍ Poster board
❍ Marker
❍ Pens
❍ Paper

This trivia game requires a little bit of research to prepare. You will need to choose at least twenty celebrities of all ages and types of acting or music. Cut out a photo of a celebrity, glue it to the poster board, and write a number below the photo. Now write down, for your eyes only, several movies each actor or actress was in. For musicians, write down lyrics from songs they have performed.

When your guests arrive, have them take a seat in front of the celebrity poster board. Hand each player a pen and paper. You will begin by naming two films that a celebrity on the board was in, without saying the name. The players must write down the name of the celebrity and the number they have on the board. Once you have gone through each celebrity, collect the papers. The player with the most correct trivia answers wins the game.

ESSENTIAL

Always make sure that the people you are entertaining are somewhat knowledgeable about the trivia category you have chosen. Some people may be very familiar with current music or celebrities, but very unaware of classical music, for example.

Movie and Show Trivia

4 or more players

What You Need

○ Pen
○ Paper
○ Index cards

This game works best if you use an assortment of television shows and movies from all eras and types. You will need to prepare half of the index cards to be television shows and the other half to be movies. It's easier if you get two different colors of index cards. Write down a description of the show/movie on the front of the card and below the description give four options for show/movie titles. At the very bottom of the card, in small print, write which letter is the correct choice.

When your guests arrive have them sit in front of you. Go around and ask the players if they want to do show or movie trivia. Once they have chosen, pull that card, read it, and see if they can get the right answer. For every incorrect answer, you will tuck the card back into the stack without revealing the correct answer. If they get it correct, hand them the card. It's a good way to keep count of how many correct responses each person has had. The player with the most cards at the end of the game is the trivia winner.

Brain-Teasing and Puzzle Games

Brainteasers and puzzles are great for keeping people engaged. It takes a good listening ear, a keen sense of observation, and the ability to weed out the unnecessary in order to solve them. People find it quite rewarding to be able to solve something that others may struggle to understand. Good luck with the following brainteasers and puzzles!

Spoon Brainteaser

What You Need

○ Silver spoon

You and one other person will need to know how this brainteaser works to pull it off successfully. One person is the "spoon photographer" and the other person is the "mind reader." The mind reader steps into another room. The photographer will use the spoon to "take a picture" of one of the guests' faces. Once the picture is taken, the mind reader will be called back into the room and handed the spoon. He or she will look at the spoon and stare for a moment and then reveal whose photo was taken. Continue to do this until everyone gives up or figures it out. You can even let others take a shot at being the mind reader.

The trick to this brainteaser is that the photographer has to sit in the exact same position as the person whose photo was taken. That way the mind reader can come in and, at a glance, know who the person is. If by chance the person is sitting in the same position as someone else, the mind reader will have to wait to guess until the person repositions or moves a little. This will certainly pique your guests' interest.

Crystal Clear Game

1 or more players

What You Need

○ Six clear glasses

Fill three of the glasses half full with water. Line the glasses up in a row, alternating the full and empty glasses, so that the even glasses are empty, and the odd glasses are full. The trick is to figure out how to move just one glass to make it so that three of the filled glasses are next to one another, and the three empty glasses are in a row together. Let your guests try to figure out what they would need to do to make this happen.

The answer is to pick up the fifth glass, pour the liquid into second glass, and sit the empty glass back down in the fifth spot. The first three glasses are now full and the last three are empty—goal accomplished. This one is good to do with one to two people at a time, so that if anyone gets it, few hear the answer, and others can have a shot at trying it.

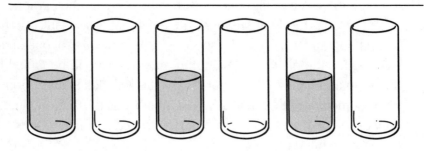

Brain Teasing Puzzles

Try these puzzles out on your guests as well:

What does this mean?

Lisa	Donna	Cheryl
	LAW	
Mike	Bill	Tim

Answer: No man is above the law

What does this mean?
I Right I

Answer: Right between the eyes

Which word could be added in between the following two words to create two new words, one starting with ARM, and the other ending with STAND?

ARM_____STAND

Answer: BAND

What does this mean?

OR NOTHING OR NOTHNG

Answer. Double or nothing

If it takes four people one hour to dig a hole in the ground, how long would it take to dig half a hole?

Answer: You can't dig half a hole

How many simple four-letter words can you make from the letters EAMN, using every letter in each word?

Answer: Four words (MEAN, NAME, AMEN, MANE)

Balloon Competition Games

Working with balloons can make for a fun game with a simple rule system: Don't pop the balloon and you have a chance at winning. Here are some great balloon games that are cost-effective and entertaining.

Balloon Waddle

2 or more players

What You Need

○ Latex balloons

To begin this game, you need to supply each player with an air-filled balloon. You also need to map out a race area that is at least twenty feet in distance, and mark a finish line. The object of the game is to for each person to place the balloon between his or her knees and hurry to cross the finish line. The first person to reach the finish line without dropping the balloon or causing it to pop becomes the winner. Players who drop their balloon must turn around and start over. If the players pop the balloon, they must go back for a new one and start over.

ALERT

As with any small items, you must always be aware of choking hazards with children under the age of five. If small children are playing any of the games in this section, make sure to keep the balloons out of their mouths and dispose of all popped balloons properly.

Balloon Keep-Away

6 or more players, in teams of 2 or more

What You Need

- ○ Balloons
- ○ String
- ○ Stopwatch

This game will keep the players on their toes at all times. Set the stopwatch to two minutes. Each player will have an air-filled balloon tied to his or her ankle. The mission is to not only try to pop the other team's balloons, but to also protect your own. Once the time is up, the team with the most balloons left wins the game.

Balloon Burglar

6 or more players

What You Need

○ Balloons

Have the players of this game get in a circle. Have someone volunteer or choose someone to stand in the middle. This person is the balloon burglar. While the players on the outside are tossing, passing, and kicking the balloon to one another, the burglar is trying to take the balloon. If the burglar captures the balloon, then the last person who touched it has to get in the middle to be the burglar. This continues for as long as you like, and if the balloon pops, you can end the game or just use another.

Balloon Word-Scramble

4 or more players

What You Need

○ Latex balloons
○ Fat-tip marker

Who would have thought balloons could be used to make you brush up on your spelling? To get this game going, you will need to inflate the balloons and write a letter on each balloon. For the vowels, you'll want to do several of each, and make more of the letters R, S, T, D, M, and N. When all of the balloons are prepared, scatter them all on the floor and separate your guests into teams.

Each team will run in and pick six random balloons and go back to their area. They now have three minutes to come up with as many words as they can using the letters they picked. For each word they make, they have to show you to verify the word and for you to tally their points. They will do three rounds. Whichever team has accumulated the most points by the end of the game wins.

CHAPTER 4

Summer Vacation Games

Summer vacation is a special time for your kids (and you), which is why you want to make sure that you fill it with as much fun and laughter as possible. A great way to do this is to be prepared with a variety of games that are perfect for every situation during your summer break!

Backyard Summer Games

Everyone anticipates the coming of summer and all the fun that is at hand. Your best bet is to be prepared with a variety of games that are perfect for every situation you and your kids might encounter.

Whether it's fun in the sun or water games, being outside on a hot summer day is an adventure in itself. Adding a few fun games to the mix will get everyone's mind on playing and not sweating. The best part about this selection of games is that you won't need a lot of supplies because playing outside allows for a variety of simple, great games.

Hoop Toss

3 or more players

What You Need

- ❍ 3 Hula-Hoops
- ❍ 3 bar stools or chairs

This outdoor game is a larger version of Ring Toss. Place the bar stools or chairs randomly around the yard. Have the first player stand about ten feet from the first stool and try to toss a Hula-Hoop over the stool. Leave it wherever it lands, and give that person the next hoop. That person will try to make it over the next stool, and do the same with the last Hula-Hoop and stool. Once that person's turn has ended, gather the Hula-Hoops up and bring them back to where the players are standing so that others can try. The following players will step up, one by one, and toss the three hoops. The player to get the most Hula-Hoops around the stools—or closest to the stools—wins the game.

Steal the Bacon

2 teams of 6 or more players, and a leader

What You Need

○ Ball (a beach ball works great)

This is a great team game to play outside. Split the participants into two evenly sized teams. Each team stands in a line so the teams are facing each other, at least fifteen feet apart. Place the ball, which is known as the bacon, in the middle between the two teams.

Give each player of the first team a number, starting with the number one, and do the same for the other team. You will then call out a random number. The two players who were given that number will rush out to try and get the bacon. If a player gets the bacon without being tagged by the other person, that player will bring it back to his or her side and receive a point. If the player is tagged while holding the bacon, then no one receives a point, and the bacon goes back to the middle for the next pair of players to try for.

You may play as long as you like, or set a point amount to reach in order to end the game. The team with the most points wins.

Watermelon Seed-Spitting Contest

2 or more players (over the age of 5) and a whistle blower

What You Need

○ Watermelon seeds
○ Whistle

The next time you enjoy a nice juicy watermelon, save those little seeds! This game is simple and fun for everyone. You will need to have an area with a light-colored ground, like concrete. You can even lay down a large white garbage bag or tarp if you like, just to make sure that you can see the seeds after they are spit out.

In this game, participants put seeds in their mouth, and when the whistle is blown, they spit the seeds as far as they can. Make sure to have everyone stand a couple feet from each other, or go one at a time and find a way to identify each player's seed, so that the seeds are not mixed up. The person whose seed lands the farthest away wins the competition.

QUESTION

My child has an allergy to watermelon; is there another seed that can be used?
Apple seeds have a similar weight and color to watermelon seeds, so they will work just fine. Pumpkin seeds also work, because they are bigger than most seeds.

Centipede Hustle

12 or more players separated into 2 teams

All you need for this hilarious game are two teams that are ready to work together. Set a point as the starting line and a point as the finishing line. Assign each person to a team, and have each person line up one after the other. Each team will have to move as one to win this game.

When the race starts, the players will quickly sit down and wrap their legs around the team member directly in front of them. They should position their legs tightly so they can remain locked during the hustle to the finish line. They are to lift their bodies using their arms and push forward as a team. If the centipede comes apart, the team must stop and reconnect. The first full centipede to cross the finish line is the winner of the Centipede Hustle!

Water Balloon Games

Water balloons are a classic way to cool down from the hot weather, and it just so happens that laughter usually follows closely behind! The next set of games will get everyone tossing water balloons around in a water-filled frenzy. Just make sure that any broken balloon pieces are quickly cleaned up if you have young children under five at the party.

Water Balloon Hunt

6 or more players separated into 2 teams

What You Need

- ○ Lots of water balloons (at least a couple dozen), filled up in advance
- ○ A bucket for each team

This is very much like an egg hunt, but with water balloons. Hide the water balloons all over the area you are playing the game in. Separate the players into two teams, and assign each team a bucket and a home station. Once the game starts, each team has five minutes to find as many water balloons as possible and put them in their bucket. Once the five minutes are up, the teams can launch an attack on each other with their collected balloons!

Water Balloon Scramble

4 or more players separated into 2 teams

What You Need

- ○ At least one pre-filled water balloon per player (though you can have more)
- ○ Cotton twine or yarn (preferably in two different colors)

Any age group can play this game, because it's just great fun! Separate the players into two teams. Have each player tie a "belt" around his or her waist made from the cotton twine or yarn. The best way to play the game is to have two different colors of twine or yarn, and assign a color to each team, because this game can get moving pretty fast, and the different colors make it easier to remember who is on your team.

Tie one or more filled water balloons around each player's waist on the cotton twine or yarn, making sure each player has the same number of balloons. Have the teams stand opposite each other. When someone yells "Go," the teams will try to pop all the balloons on the belts of the opposite team. It's best to only let this go on for about three minutes. Once the time is up, have the players return to their sides. Do a balloon count, and the team with the most remaining balloons is the winner.

FACT

Rubber balloons were invented by a man named Michael Faraday back in 1824. Before that, balloons were made from animal intestines. Water balloons and birthday balloons were one of the first uses for rubber balloons. Without Mr. Faraday, water balloon fights would be a lot less common and entertaining!

Fragile-Package Toss

An even number of 4 or more players separated into teams of 2

What You Need

○ One pre-filled water balloon for each team

Have everyone pick a partner, and give one water balloon to each pair. Have all the pairs line up in a row, partners facing one another. The object of the game is to toss the water balloon back and forth between partners without breaking it. Each time players catch the balloon, they have to take a step backward before tossing it back to their partner. The last team with an unpopped water balloon wins the game!

Cannonballs and Treasure

5 or more players

What You Need

○ Several black water balloons (at least 10)
○ Several dry beans, 1 for each balloon
○ String
○ A tree with branches low enough to hang the water balloons on

○ "Treasure" (as many little prizes as you have beans and water balloons)

When preparing the balloons, insert a dry bean on the inside of each one before filling it with water. These are "magic" beans that can later be traded for treasure! Hang each balloon, or "cannonball," from a string in the tree, measuring different lengths based on the guests' heights. The mission is to retrieve the balloons, pop them, and find the magic beans. Once all the balloons are popped, the players can trade the beans in for "treasure."

Pool Party Games

Though not everyone owns a pool, there are public pools, indoor and outdoor, in most cities. Swimming around and just lounging in the water can be fun all on its own, but sometimes a game is needed to get the laughter flowing. These pool games bring the party into the water.

Noodle Jousting

4 or more players

What You Need

○ 4 or more pool noodles (1 for each player)
○ 4 or more water rafts (1 for each player)

Though this game is quite simple, it can become very competitive and addicting. Start by giving each person a pool noodle and a raft. Start with two players, each sitting on his or her raft in the water, and when the game starts, they must try to knock each other off the rafts using the noodles. The winning player from each joust will go on to joust the next person in line, until he or she is defeated. The person with the most wins at the end is the noodle-jousting champion.

Colors

4 or more players

Ask one of the players to volunteer to be "It," or a leader can assign someone to be "It." The person who is "It" will stand facing away from the rest of the players near the edge of the pool. The players will line up in the water with their hands against the wall of the pool directly behind the person who is "It," and secretly assign themselves a color that no one else knows.

The person who is "It" will start to call out colors, and if a swimmer's color is called, that person must try to quietly swim to the other side of the pool. If by chance the person playing "It" hears this, he or she can jump or dive in and try to tag the swimmer. If the swimmer is tagged, then that person becomes "It." However, if "It" turns around and all the swimmers still have their hands on the side of the pool, "It" must take a step away from the pool.

ALERT

Whenever you are playing games in a pool, of course, you want to take precautions to avoid any rough play or possibilities of drowning. Having the younger children wear floaters or having an adult in the pool will help to avoid any issues for the little ones or those that can't swim so well.

Treasure Dive

3 or more players

What You Need

○ Lots of small-to-medium-size items that sink in water
○ A bucket or bowl for each player

This game works best when played in a large in-ground pool, but can still be played in most other pools. Have each player place his or her bowl or bucket outside of the pool but still within reach. Toss all the items into the pool, making sure to scatter them on the floor of the pool.

When the game begins, the players jump in the pool and begin gathering the items—one at a time!—and putting them in their bowls or buckets.

If anyone is caught gathering more than one item at a time, he or she will be disqualified from the game. The game continues until all the pieces have been collected from the floor of the pool. The player with the most items at the end of the treasure dive wins the game. You can also allow the players to keep the items they collect as party favors.

Octopus

4 or more players

Begin by choosing someone to be the octopus. The octopus stays in the middle of the pool, and the swimmers on the outer parts of the pool have to try to swim past him or her to the other side without being tagged. The swimmers who are tagged will hold hands with the octopus and then have to help tag others. You can keep this up until you are down to one last swimmer and start over with a new octopus.

Luau Party Games

You don't have to live on an island to have a luau. You can very easily bring the Hawaiian Islands to your party. On top of doing the hula and the limbo, here are a few games that will get the Hawaiian party started!

Pass the Mango

6 or more players separated into teams

What You Need

○ Mangoes (1 per team)

This is a great luau game that involves teamwork. The players will tuck a mango under their chin and shoulder, race over to their teammates, and pass the mango to them without any use of their hands. If the mango is dropped, it can be picked up and put back in between the player's shoulder and chin, but then the team must start back over with the first person. The first team to pass the mango around without dropping it wins.

'Ulu Maika

3 or more players

What You Need

❍ 2 wooden stakes that can be pounded into the ground (like croquet stakes)
❍ Medium-size stone

'Ulu Maika is an authentic Hawaiian lawn game. What better time to play it than at a luau? Pound the two wooden stakes into the ground about six inches apart. The players will stand at least twelve feet back from the stakes. The object of the game is to roll the stone in between the two wooden stakes. Seems simple enough, but this game actually takes patience and concentration.

FACT

Luaus are known for traditional island dancers and delicious food. The most common food served at a Hawaiian luau is Kalua pork. The pig was traditionally cooked in an imu, an underground oven, but now it is more commonly roasted in a fire pit and enjoyed by all who attend.

Tour-the-Islands Toss

4 or more players

What You Need

○ Large trashcan
○ Raffia material
○ Ball
○ A printout of each Hawaiian island

To set up the game you will need to wrap the raffia material around the large trashcan. Place the island cutouts around the base of the trashcan, around two feet from the can, in a U shape. Now have the players line up behind the first island and try to toss the ball into the can. If they make it in, then they can move on to the next island and take that shot. This will continue until the player misses, in which case the ball goes to the next person. The first person to make it all the way through the islands wins.

Lei Relay Race

6 or more players

What You Need

○ Cheap plastic leis
○ Hula-Hoops

Split the players into teams, give each team a Hula-Hoop, and place it on the ground. Dump about twenty leis inside each hoop. When someone yells "Go," the first person of each team has to run over to the piles of leis, put one on, and run back to the team. The person then has to take off the lei and put it on the next player in line. This player has to run over and grab another lei, put it on, and run back to the team. That player then takes off both leis and puts them on the next person. This process continues until all of the leis are collected on a player's neck. The team to complete the task first wins.

Summer Preschool Games (Ages 3–5)

Venturing outside with preschool-aged children can turn into a game of chase-the-tots if you don't have a plan in place. Most preschoolers are very curious and love to interact with others as well as their environment. The following games should keep your preschooler very busy.

Shark Attack

4 or more players

What You Need

- ○ Small pool
- ○ Bag of balloons
- ○ Permanent fat-tip marker

Most little ones love getting wet, especially if they are not supposed to. Luckily, this game allows them to get wet while staying out of trouble. Blow up about ten balloons and draw shark fins and faces on them. Make sure there is water in the pool and put the balloons in. On "Go," the children will jump in and try to squish the sharks by sitting on them. The person to squish the most sharks wins the game.

ALERT

When preschool children are outside playing in the sun, it is very easy for them to become dehydrated. It is important to take frequent water breaks. Wearing a good sunscreen is the best way to avoid any burns. It is also a good idea to let them sit in a shaded area when taking their drink breaks to help them cool off a bit.

Spongy Feet

8 or more players

What You Need

- ○ Large sponges
- ○ Buckets of water

This game can get a little wet, but it is definitely a fun way to cool off on a summer day. Divide the children into two teams, and have all of the players lie down next to one another so that their feet are next to someone's head and vice versa. Put the bucket of water at the starting point of each team. Have the first players dip the sponge into the water using their feet.

They must now pass it to the people next to them without dropping it and they must do the same, using only their feet, down the line until it reaches the end and comes back. If the sponge is dropped, it can only be picked up using the feet. The first team to get the sponge down and back and into the bucket wins the game.

Coconut Bowling

3 or more players

What You Need

○ Coconut or a ball painted like one
○ Empty 2-liter bottles

Begin this cute summer game by setting up the two-liter bottles like you would pins at a bowling alley. If you are playing with an actual coconut, you might want to put a little bit of water in each two-liter bottle to add a little weight to them. Have the preschoolers take turns rolling the ball and trying to knock over as many bottles as they can. The child with the most pins knocked down after a couple of rounds wins the game.

Summer Kids' Games (Ages 6–9)

Summer games for a kid are usually centered on video games or cartoon watching. It's easy to ignore the shining sun and warm weather when they're inside, unaware of fun they could be having outside. Getting them to go outside can be easy if there are games to play! There's nothing like a good game outside to make sitting on the couch seem boring.

Musical Beach Towels

4 or more players

What You Need

❍ Beach towel for each person, except 1
❍ Music

Have each child lay down a beach towel in front of him or her. You should have one towel less than the number of children participating. Start playing the music and have the children dance around the towels. You will periodically stop the music so that the children have to rush to sit down on a towel. The last one to sit down is out.

You will now take a towel away and start the music again. Each time someone is disqualified, take a towel away until there is only one towel left. The last two children will compete to sit down first. The person to sit on the last beach towel is the winner of the game.

Chalky Target

4 or more players

What You Need

❍ Chalk
❍ Kitchen sponges
❍ Bucket filled with water

Draw a large target on the concrete with the chalk. Inside the center ring of the target, draw a 3 for three points; in the next ring, draw a 2 for two points; and in the outer ring, put the number 1 for one point. Put the bucket next to the starting line, which should be about five feet away from the target. Place sponges in the water to let them soak.

Have the children line up and grab a sponge from the bucket, then have them toss the sponge toward the target to see how many points they can hit. Have them rotate around so they can try at least two times. If you have a small group of children, you might let them try at least three times. The one with the most points at the end is the winner.

Volleyball Splash

2 or more players

What You Need

○ Small pool
○ Large sponge

Have the players stand on opposite sides of the pool facing one another. The first person will pick up the wet sponge and serve it, like a volleyball, to the other player. The object of the game is to keep the sponge in the air. If it lands on the ground, the player(s) who did not touch the sponge last get(s) a point. If it lands in the pool, the last one to touch it loses a point. The first to win ten points has conquered the game.

Summer Tween Games (Ages 10–12)

When kids hit the ten- or eleven-year-old mark, they tend to leave behind a lot of child's play. They are now trying to act a little cooler and more sophisticated. Because of this, it is sometimes hard to get them involved in family activities or games. Don't worry—these summer games will do the trick in no time!

Back-to-Back Balloon Dash

6 or more players

What You Need

○ Water balloons

Water balloons are great on a summer day, and playing a game where you try not to pop one may sound odd, but it is very funny to watch. Set a point for the start of the race and for the finish line. Have the players split up into teams of two, and hand out one water balloon to each team. The object of the game is to have the players stand back to back and place a water balloon between the two of their backs. They must make it to the designated finish line without popping their balloon in order to win. If the balloon pops, then they have to start all over again.

ESSENTIAL

Any summer game in this section can be turned into a water game by swapping water balloons for the balls. Tweens love to cool off from a warm day outside just as much as younger kids, so why not change the game up and surprise them with water play?

Homemade Ball Toss

3 or more players

What You Need

- ○ A tarp
- ○ Scissors
- ○ Paint
- ○ Ball
- ○ Nylon rope

This game is one that you can play over and over again. First, you must prepare the target. Lay the tarp out flat and cut four holes big enough for a football to go through. Paint around the outside of the cutouts and mark one with 5 points, one with 10 points, one with 15 points, and one with 20 points. While this is drying, you can cut four lengths of nylon rope to hang the tarp with. If there aren't any grommets already on the tarp, you can cut a hole in each corner and run the rope through.

Once everything is dry, hang the tarp and let the participants take turns trying to throw the ball through the holes for points. It's best to base the distance from the target on the player's age. So if a younger child is playing, he or she can stand much closer than an adult would stand. The player with the most points at the end wins the game.

Jug Master

4 or more players

What You Need

○ Duct tape
○ Empty milk jugs
○ Balls (whiffle balls or plastic balls work well) or water balloons

This game can be played with balls or with water balloons. It just depends on what you prefer for that day. You will need to cut the milk jugs in half horizontally. Keep the half that has the handle and flip it upside down. If you are planning to use water balloons, you will need to cover the edges with duct tape so that the balloons won't pop.

Give each player a jug and have him or her partner up with someone. Have the players start by standing across from one another, face-to-face. Place one ball in one of the teams' jugs. They will then toss the ball between them using their jugs. Each time someone catches it, he or she has to step backward one step and to the side. This continues until the ball is dropped or the balloon breaks. The team that is farthest apart at the end wins the game.

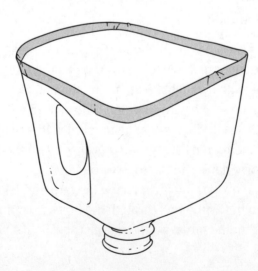

Summer Teen Games (Ages 13 and Up)

Being a teen in the summer months is all about lounging in the sun and having fun with friends. Keep some of these games in the back of your mind the next time your teen says, "I'm bored. There's nothing to do!"

Slippery Dash

6 or more players

What You Need

- ❍ 4 buckets
- ❍ Dish soap
- ❍ Plastic sheeting (a tarp would work as well)
- ❍ Hose
- ❍ 2 plastic cups
- ❍ Yard stakes

Lay out your plastic sheeting and put a yard stake in each corner to keep it posted to the ground. You need to make it nice and slippery using the dish soap and hose. Once it is ready to go, place two empty buckets at one end and two water-filled buckets at the other end. Have the players split up into two teams and tell them to line up next to the bucket with the water in it. Hand a plastic cup to the first player in each line.

When the game begins, the players must fill their cup and race across the slippery tarp to the other side. When they get to the other side, they need to dump the water into the bucket. They will then rush back to the other side and hand the cup to the next player on their team. Depending on how many players you have, you can play until everyone has had two turns or you can play until one team has filled their bucket up.

Bucket Guard

6 or more players

What You Need

O Buckets
O Plastic or foam baseball bat
O Water balloons or plastic balls
O Large tub

Have the players split up into two teams. One team will be the bucket guard and the other team will be the infiltrators. The object of the game is for the infiltrators to get as many water balloons or balls into the buckets while the bucket guards are swinging the bats to try to keep them out of the buckets.

Hand each bucket guard a bat and a bucket to sit at his or her feet. Now place a large tub of water balloons or balls behind the infiltrators. The infiltrators must stand at least eight to ten feet from the buckets. When someone yells "Go," the players will begin tossing and guarding, depending on which team they are on. The person to get the most balloons or balls into the buckets wins. The next round, the guards switch places with the infiltrators.

Broom Spin-and-Dodge

3 or more players

What You Need

O Broom
O Water balloons
O Tub for water balloons

Begin this game by designating a safe zone. You will need one person to volunteer to be the spinner and the rest will be the attackers. The spinner will take the broom, put his or her forehead to the top of the handle, and spin around five times. The spinner must then run across the yard and dodge the water balloons being tossed at him or her until reaching the safe zone.

After reaching the safe zone, someone will switch places with the spinner, and the old spinner becomes an attacker. It's best to keep it up until everyone has had at least one turn. The ones who make it without being hit by a water balloon win a prize.

CHAPTER 5

Truth-or-Dare Games

Truth or Dare is a classic party game that can help your guests get to know one another. Since it gives every participant a choice, this is a great game for both rowdy groups and shy groups. Choose "truth," and you have to answer a question in front of the group. Choose "dare," and you may be asked to do something you never imagined doing! So open up, and indulge in a good old game of Truth or Dare.

Girls' Truth or Dare

It seems that young girls always have a blast when they get together to play. Why not create even more giggles with a classic game of Truth or Dare? It's a great way to get young children to feel comfortable and share things about themselves with their peers.

Twenty-Five Girl Truth Questions

- What was the most embarrassing thing to ever happen to you?
- If someone made a movie about your life, whom would you want to play you?
- Name a secret about yourself that no one has ever known.
- Have you ever worn something that you hated, but everyone else was wearing it too?
- Reveal an embarrassing celebrity crush.
- What are you most scared of?
- Name a movie that makes you cry.
- What food do you eat at home that you like the least?
- Name three things about yourself that you like.
- Would you rather eat a worm or drink rotten milk?
- What do you do when you are angry with someone?
- Have you ever cheated on a test?
- If you could choose to be able fly or be invisible, which would you pick?
- What is the meanest thing you have ever done?
- Would you rather swim with a shark or experience a tornado?
- Where would you live if you could live anywhere in the world?
- What song best describes your life right now?
- What is the worst habit you have?
- If you could become any animal, which would you choose and why?
- Do you still (or have you ever) slept with a stuffed animal?
- If you had twenty-four hours to do anything you want, what would you do?
- If you could change one thing about your best friend, what would it be?

- Would you rather kiss a fish or a frog?
- Who is your favorite cartoon character?
- What do you want to be when you grow up?

Twenty-Five Girl Dares

- Stuff marshmallows in your mouth and sing a nursery rhyme.
- Put your clothes on backward and walk backward around the room.
- Tell everyone the funniest joke you know.
- Sniff everyone's feet in the room.
- Sing a part of your favorite song in the funniest voice you can.
- Do your makeup like a clown and stay that way for an hour.
- Try to peel a banana with your feet.
- Imitate a cartoon character until someone can guess who you are.
- Pretend you are a chicken for the next thirty seconds.
- Turn to the person next to you and smell her feet.
- Eat several pieces of bubblegum and blow a huge bubble.
- Take a bite out of an onion as if it were an apple.
- Go outside and sing a lullaby as loudly as possible.
- Take a bite out of a cat treat.
- Act like a caveman for the next ten minutes.
- Pretend you are riding a horse around the room.
- Act like you are a monkey and go around picking imaginary bugs off of people and eating them.
- Do your makeup while wearing a blindfold.
- Eat a spoonful of peanut butter and say the pledge of allegiance.
- Let someone tickle you for one minute.
- Draw a picture of someone in the room and see if anyone can guess who it is.
- Dance like a ballerina while you are drinking a glass of water.
- Spin in a circle four times and then try to walk in a straight line across the room.
- Go to the fridge, close your eyes, and point to anything inside, and then eat whatever you pointed to.
- Chew a bunch of crackers and try to whistle.

Are all truth-or-dare games embarrassing for the people playing them?
Truth or Dare is a way for players to laugh not only at each other but also at themselves, in a healthy way. Dares can sometimes help people realize how brave they are and what they are capable of. As for truths, it's often reassuring to see that others may have experienced the same embarrassing things you have.

Boys' Truth or Dare

Boys love a good truth-or-dare game just as much as girls. Most young boys already enjoy joking around with one another, so take the laughter to new heights with a truth-or-dare game that will keep them in stitches.

Twenty-Five Boy Truth Questions

- If you were stuck on an island and could only have one person with you, who would it be?
- Whom do you have a crush on?
- What is the worst gift you have ever gotten?
- If you could have a superpower, what would it be?
- What is the funniest thing to ever happen to you?
- What do you like most about the person next to you?
- Name the grossest thing you have ever eaten.
- If you could be invisible, what would you do first?
- Have you ever done a prank call, and if so, who was it to?
- Describe the scariest dream you have ever had.
- If you had to describe yourself as a food, which food would it be?
- Have you ever cried during a movie? If so, which one?
- If you could have anything in the world, what would it be?
- Have you ever been mean to someone for no reason at all?
- If you could change your name to anything you wanted, what would you choose?

- Have you ever tried to show off for a girl and it went wrong?
- Have you ever pretended to like something because a girl liked the same thing?
- What is the longest time you have gone without brushing your teeth?
- Do you sing in the shower?
- Have you ever eaten a booger?
- Would you rather gargle toilet water or dance with your mom in front of your friends?
- Do you have a nickname that your family calls you? If so, what is it?
- Would you eat a spoonful of dirt for twenty dollars?
- Have you ever stolen anything before?
- If you had to eat a bug or lick a shoe, which would you choose?

Twenty-Five Boy Dares

- Sing "I'm a Little Teapot" while acting out the song.
- Snort like a pig at the beginning and end of each sentence for the next thirty minutes.
- Tuck your shirt in, put an ice cube down your shirt, and leave it until it melts.
- Dance without any music for the next three minutes.
- Paint your nails.
- Eat a spoonful of mustard in one bite.
- Perform a cheer just like a cheerleader would.
- Eat a bowl of cereal from the floor like a dog.
- Let the person next to you draw a tattoo on your arm—his choice of design.
- Eat several sheets of toilet paper.
- Pretend the person next to you is the girl you like and ask "her" out on a date.
- Talk continuously for two minutes straight.
- Crabwalk across the room and back to where you started without falling.
- Toss an egg high in the air and try to catch it without breaking it.
- Put your socks on your hands and wear them like that for ten minutes.

- Act out a scene from your favorite movie, but use a high-pitched voice the whole time.
- Jump in the shower with all your clothes on.
- Stuff as many marshmallows as you possibly can in your mouth.
- Say the alphabet backward while doing jumping jacks.
- Pretend you are a sumo wrestler and challenge someone in the room to a match.
- Cover your chin in peanut butter and let a dog lick it off.
- Pretend to be a girl, voice and all, for the next ten minutes.
- Dance like you are at a disco party.
- Let the person next to you pick an animal. You must act like that animal until it is your turn again.
- Go next door and ask the neighbor to borrow some toilet paper.

ALERT

Anytime a child is directed to leave the safety of home to complete a dare, it is best to have an adult stay close by, especially if the child is not familiar with the area or neighborhood.

Kids' Truth or Dare

You always have the classic game of Truth or Dare to play; however, mixing things up a bit and changing the rules can always be entertaining. This will keep them curious. The following are ways to alter the game when there is a mix of kids playing.

Boys vs. Girls

Have the girls and boys separate into teams. For each truth that is answered the team gets one point, and for each dare the team gets two points. If a person wants to switch from truth to dare after the question has been asked, he or she will only receive one point for the dare. If anyone refuses to complete a truth or dare, the team loses one point. The team with the most points at the end wins.

Truth or Dare, Double Dare, Triple Dare

Instead of having just a dare, you can come up with some double dares or triple dares. The double dares should be something they have to do with a partner or something that is kind of gross. For example, you could double dare someone to lick the bottom of a shoe as a gross dare. A triple dare is something that would be very embarrassing or extremely gross. For example, you could triple dare someone to hold a worm for thirty seconds or put on clown makeup and honk everyone's nose.

Tween and Teen Truth or Dare

A lot of the time, people avoid truth-or-dare games for this age range because they are afraid it will turn into something they are trying to stay away from. Sometimes this game is nixed because teens find it to be repetitive. Here are some games to avoid both of those issues.

Never Have I Ever

Hand everyone three pennies to use as scorekeepers. The first person starts by saying, "Never have I ever . . ." and then says something he or she has never done before. For example, players could say, "Never have I ever been on an airplane," "Never have I ever swam in a public pool," "Never have I ever lied to my parents," and "Never have I ever eaten broccoli." All of the players who *have* done that thing forfeit a penny.

When the next person goes, he or she will offer another example. If someone runs out of pennies, he or she must then do a dare in order to gain three pennies back. The player or players with the most pennies win(s) the game. To avoid this game becoming inappropriate, just set the ground rule that all comments need to be clean and suitable for all ears.

Truth or Dare Pass

With this variation, players draw a paper out of a bag, and read the truth or dare out loud. The player has the choice of answering the question, completing the dare, or passing it on to someone else in the group. That person now has to complete the truth or dare, and if he or she refuses, that person is out.

Adult Truth or Dare

Adult Truth or Dare doesn't always have to be on the awkward end of the spectrum. Here are twenty-five questions and twenty-five dares that will embarrass some people but not make them want to crawl under a rock.

Truths

- What food is your guilty pleasure?
- What is the last lie you told?
- Have you ever broken the law, and what was it that you did?
- Who was the first person you had a crush on, and how old were you?
- If you could spend the day with anyone, dead or alive, who would it be?
- What are your three biggest pet peeves?
- Who is your favorite family member?
- Do you ever lie about your income, and if so, do you inflate or deflate the amount?
- What about you makes you the most self-conscious?
- What was the worst breakup you have ever experienced?

- Have you ever dated more than one person at a time?
- What is the scariest thing that has ever happened to you?
- What is one of your best memories?
- If you had to be a character out of a movie or book, who would you be?
- What's the biggest lie you have ever told?
- If you could live anywhere in the world, where would you move?
- Who is your celebrity crush?
- What is your biggest flaw?
- What was the worst date you ever went on?
- Would you leave your partner for a million dollars?
- If you could only eat one meal for the rest of your life, what would it be?
- If you had only three days left on earth, what would you do with the rest of your time?
- Do you have any talents no one knows about?
- If you had to switch lives with a person in the room, with whom would you switch?
- What is the thing you like least about your partner?

ALERT

Before starting a game of Truth or Dare with adults, it is always good to lay some ground rules so that everyone is on the same page. This helps to avoid any issues of players being asked extremely uncomfortable questions.

Dares

- Pretend you are a fashion designer and point out the dos and don'ts of fashion by using the people in the room as examples.
- Draw a mustache on your face with a marker.
- Do the best split that you can.
- Pretend to break up with the person next to you.

- Choose a random person in the room; sit on that person's lap and refuse to get up.
- Make a diaper out of toilet paper and wear it for the rest of the game.
- Give someone in the room a piggyback ride.
- Create a rap that involves each person in the room.
- Wear your shoes on your hands for the next twenty minutes.
- Act out a scene from one of your favorite movies.
- Let the person next to you do your makeup while that person is blindfolded.
- With your eyes closed, spin around in a circle five times and then try to run around the room.
- Use an accent of your choice for the next hour, and if you forget, you have to start over.
- Call a family member and ask him (or her) if he (or she) believes in aliens and hang up.
- Give someone in the room a foot massage.
- Try to lick your elbow.
- Dance like a ballerina.
- Serenade the person next to you.
- Convince someone to let you give him or her butterfly kisses with your eyelashes.
- Wear a "Kick me" sign on your back for an hour.
- Wrap your arms around yourself and slow dance.
- Go ask the neighbors if they have seen your missing lion that got loose somehow.
- Lick salt off of the back of someone's hand.
- Smile the whole time you are telling a really sad story—you cannot laugh.
- Assign nicknames to everyone in the room.

Office Truth or Dare

Just because you are at work doesn't mean you can't enjoy a playful game of Truth or Dare. Two or more employees can play this quietly, so no one else will know why you are acting funny, or the entire office group can play it. Here are some truths and dares to help get the game in gear.

Office Truths

- Do you have a crush on anyone in the office?
- Have you ever pretended to be sick to avoid a deadline or workday?
- If you won the lottery and were going to quit, how would you do it?
- What would you change about where you work?
- What is the most embarrassing thing to happen to you at work?
- If you could switch jobs with anyone in the office, who would it be?

According to recent studies of the workplace, playing games can increase not only productivity, but office morale as well. If you take a break and kick back every once in a while at work, you will find yourself working more efficiently and feeling happier. Bring on the games, right?

Office Dares

- Sit in a chair and hold, then point, an opened stapler, like speed radar, at passing employees and yell, "Slow down!"
- Give everyone in the office wrestling names.
- For the next hour, refer to every male employee as Bob and every female employee as Barb.
- Run, full speed, around the office two times.
- Stand up, put your hand over your heart, and recite the Pledge of Allegiance.
- Start a conversation with another employee not playing the game, and then just walk off when the person is talking.
- Walk sideways everywhere you go for the rest of the workday.
- Stare at the top corner of the room with a full-blown look of fear; when someone asks you what's wrong, scream, then calmly say, "What are you talking about?"
- Whenever you speak to another employee, repeat everything that you say two times, imitating an echo.

- Cry like a baby every time someone says the word "yesterday" and jump up and down if someone mentions the word "tomorrow."
- Smile the biggest smile you can every time someone approaches you, then drop your head and sob when he or she walks away.
- Go around the office and ask to borrow one thing from each person you pass. When you are done, return items to the wrong people, but stick with the idea that the item is what you borrowed from them no matter what they say.
- Draw a picture of each person in the office, and give it to him or her as a gift, asking that person to hang it up or display it in his or her area.
- When someone says your name, crow like a rooster and flap your arms.
- Get on a rolling chair and have someone push you down a hallway while you shout, "My brakes are out!"

Family Truth or Dare

How much do you *really* know about your family members? The best way to find out is to play a game of Truth or Dare. The classic game can be altered in a couple of ways to keep things interesting. Here are a few of the altered versions of the game.

Family vs. Family Truth or Dare

If you know a family that you would love to take on in a game of Truth or Dare, this is how you can do it. To keep track of who is winning, be sure to keep a chart for points. Give one point for truths completed by a family member, and two points if everyone in the family answers that truth; three points for a dare being completed by a family member, and five points if the entire family completes the dare. The family with the most points at the end wins.

Penalty-Juice Family Truth or Dare

This version of Truth or Dare is best played if there are questions that have gone unanswered, like "Who really broke that window?" or "Do you really brush your teeth every night?" As a bonus to this game, there is a "penalty juice" involved. It consists of using any condiments or drinks out of the fridge and concocting a juice players have to try if they refuse to answer a truth directed at them.

Have everyone write down his or her truths before the game begins. It's best to set a number of truths for each family member. Three is usually a good number per member. As the game begins, one person will ask a truth he or she wrote down for a certain person; if the person answers, then that person takes a turn. If the person refuses and opts for a dare, then he or she must try the penalty juice and take the dare.

If the person refuses the dare, the entire family of the opposite team must come up with a dare that person must do in order to stay in the game. If the person refuses that dare, her or she is out of the game. The family with the most players still in the game at the end wins. If you are playing with an uneven number of players, you can go by how many were lost rather than how many are remaining.

ESSENTIAL

A good penalty-juice recipe would be a little pickle juice, grapefruit juice, mustard, chocolate syrup, and paprika mixed together in a glass. One little taste of this stuff will get everyone to answer those truth questions in an instant!

Chore-Duty Family Truth or Dare

Children and parents love this version of the game because it helps motivate everyone to do his or her chores. In this game, for each truth that is given, the person asking can offer a dare up for a chore trade.

For example, if you accept a dare, before the other person reveals what it is, you have to offer up a chore, like washing dishes for two days. If the person accepts and you do the dare, he or she must do said chore. It's best to write down what the chores are and who has to do them. In the meantime, you get to enjoy watching your family get silly.

CHAPTER 6

Treasure and Scavenger Hunts

Treasure hunts and scavenger hunts are incredibly flexible activities. They can be quick or last for hours, depending how complex you make them. Hunts are also good for restless people of all ages, because they are able to run around and solve challenges. Not to mention there's no greater feeling than finally finding the prize at the end of the game! Here are several types of ideas for treasure and scavenger hunts that can be altered to fit any theme or situation.

Preschoolers' Hunts

People often think that preschool-aged children lack the mental capacity to be able participate in a hunt, yet preschoolers are actually very observant when the hunt involves things that interest them. The following hunts are ideal for preschoolers, so give them some credit and a little bit of time, and they will surprise you!

Nature's Color Hunt

2 or more players

What You Need

○ Glue sticks and tape
○ Scissors
○ Markers
○ Poster board
○ Plastic bag for each child

Start by cutting out a circle for each child from white poster board. Around the edges of the cutout, draw ten circles. Using the markers, color a patch inside each circle. The colors are as follows: white, black, brown, red, pink, orange, yellow, green, blue, and purple. As the children arrive, hand each one a cutout and a plastic bag. The children should then go outside and try to find items that are the colors that are on their boards. When they are done, they have to go inside and glue or tape the items onto their circle cutouts. You can add silver and gold as bonuses, but these are always hard to find.

ALERT

Make sure that an adult is available to assist the preschoolers during Nature's Color Hunt. Some adults may need to even hold the plastic bags for tots so that there is no risk of them placing them in their mouths or over their heads.

At-the-Park Scavenger Hunt

2 or more players

What You Need

- ○ Plastic bags
- ○ Cheap stuffed animals or animals printed on paper

This hunt is great for a trip to the park, or it can even be played in your backyard! Since the younger children (toddlers) are not yet familiar with reading, it is best to use pictures to symbolize what they need to find during a hunt.

Start by printing out pictures of all types of animals. Make a list for the children to share and then give them a bag. You can purchase some cheap little stuffed animals from a dollar store, or print animal pictures, to use for hiding.

You will also need to write clues to lead the children to the animals after you hide them. For example, if you want them to find a squirrel, you could tell the kids that the squirrel loves to hide in the branches of a . . . and let them guess the answer and lead you to it. For a monkey, you could say he loves to play on these bars that are named after him.

Go around the park, without the children seeing you, and hide the animals in the spots based on your clues. An adult should accompany the children on the hunt to help with clues and discovery. Once they have found all the animals, you can reward them with a treat or a small prize.

Sandbox Hunt

4 or more players

What You Need

- ○ Sandbox
- ○ Variety of little toys
- ○ Poster board

- ○ Tape
- ○ Small shovel-and-bucket sets (1 for each child)

You can do this hunt with a readymade sandbox or make one yourself by using an empty kiddie pool filled with sand. You will need to hide several different little plastic toys in the sand. It is best to make note of each toy you put in and to make sure there are enough so that every child will end up with one of each toy. Put a poster board up near the sandbox that includes an example of each toy, so the kids know what to look for.

Supply the children with a small plastic shovel and bucket to dig with. When the hunt begins, they will dig through the sand and locate one of each of the toys on the board. When they find all of them, they get to keep the toys as a prize. This is also a great way to give out the grab bags that are used as parting gifts at the end of a party.

Kids' Hunts

Not all hunts have to be a pirate-like treasure hunt. They can be altered to suit any theme. Some good themes such as army, princess, cars, and holiday work very well for a treasure hunt. Just adjust each hint to your theme. The hunt itself, not the hunt's theme, is the exciting part, so why not try them all?

The Candy Hunt

4 or more players

What You Need

- ○ Candy from list below
- ○ Paper
- ○ Marker
- ○ Tape

Everyone knows that finding sweet treats on a scavenger hunt is the best. In this hunt, each clue will have its own location. Each clue will be a candy slogan, and each participant will need to name the candy it belongs to and locate that candy. The clue should be written on a piece of paper and attached to the candy. Here is the slogan list:

Slogan	Candy Brand
Taste the rainbow	Skittles
Sometimes you feel like a nut, sometimes you don't	Mounds/Almond Joy
It's all in the mix *or* Need a moment? Chew it over with a	Twix
Get the sensation	YORK Peppermint Pattie
Gimme a break, Gimme a break	KIT KAT
Melts in your mouth, not in your hand	M&Ms
How many licks does it take to get to the center?	Tootsie Pops
Isn't life juicy?	Starburst
A lighter way to enjoy chocolate	3 Musketeers
First they're sour, then they're sweet	Sour Patch Kids
There's no wrong way to eat a . . .	Reese's Peanut Butter Cup
Don't let hunger happen to you	Snickers
At work, rest, or play you get three great tastes with a . . .	Milky Way
Nobody's gonna lay a finger on my . . .	Butterfinger

FACT

Did you know that chocolate has been a popular treat for more than 3,000 years? People have enjoyed it as early as the Aztec civilization. Also, marshmallows were said to have been a tasty treat for the ancient Egyptians.

Neighborhood Hunt

6 or more players

What You Need

- ○ Paper for making lists
- ○ Pen or computer with printer for making lists
- ○ Bags for collection

First, make a list of twenty items to locate. Here's a suggested list:

- Dryer sheet
- Empty water bottle
- Clean sock
- Store receipt
- Blue flower
- Something shaped like a star
- Toy car
- Pack of sugar
- Newspaper page
- Red crayon
- A piece of plastic silverware
- Paper cup
- A candle
- Can of soup
- Picture of an animal in human clothing
- Coloring-book page, already colored
- Cotton ball
- Business card
- Battery
- Potato

Then, have the players ask trusted nearby neighbors (avoid neighbors you're not familiar with) to help out with the items on their lists. It's definitely best if children are paired into groups of at least three on each team, and an adult should accompany younger children. The list above can be altered to your liking, or kept as is for the hunt. You can also put point values on the items, as some of them will be much harder to come by. The team with the most items or points wins the hunt.

Kitchen Scavenger Hunt

3 or more players

What You Need

○ Paper

○ Marker
○ Tape

A hunt like this usually doesn't require a special shopping trip, since most of the items on the list are found in most kitchens. When doing your clues, make sure to put them somewhere on the product that the players can't see until they are picking it up. That way, they will not be able to skip through the game too quickly. The treasure at the end is the birthday cake, but this game can be altered to fit your very own treasure idea.

▼ **CLUES AND ANSWERS**

Cow juice	Milk
Sweet sand	Sugar
Both creamy and yellow, I spread nicely on bread	Butter
We sound the same, but we are spelled differently, and I don't belong in a vase	Flour
I'm squeezed from a fruit and my color is my name	Orange juice
You can mash me, fry me, or bake me	Potatoes
Most think I am a nut, but I'm really the butter of a legume	Peanut butter
I come in many flavors and am great whether cold or melted	Cheese
I'm sugary sweet, baked, and decorated for your pleasure	Birthday cake

Tween and Teen Hunts

You are really never too old to go hunting for treasure. The best way to get the older crowd involved in a hunt is to offer up something that makes them want to work to get that treasure. It can be a simple gift certificate or a new video game they may be drooling over at the moment. Offer up the bait and watch them flock in to join the hunt.

Magazine and Newspaper Hunt

4 or more players

What You Need

○ Old magazines and newspapers
○ Glue
○ Scissors
○ Paper

Get the players together to go on a hunt. If you don't personally have any old magazines, you may be able to get some old ones from libraries and doctor's offices. Give each player a list, paper to attach the findings on, scissors, glue, and some old reading material. Each player must find everything on the list, cut them out, and then paste the pictures on the paper. The player that finds all the items first wins. Here is a list of scavenger items you can use or start with:

- Glass of milk
- Soda can
- Blue eyes
- Blue necktie
- The word "simple"
- Red-haired person
- Water
- Chihuahua dog
- Cheese
- Truck
- Someone holding a baby
- Fire
- A political figure
- Road sign

Mall Scavenger Hunt

4 or more players

What You Need

○ Paper and pen, or computer with printer (to print lists)

No need to set the players loose with money in hand, just send them out in teams of at least two players each with a list of freebies to obtain, and see how far they get. A sales associate must sign by each item on the list, and players cannot retrieve more than one item per store. The person or team to return to home base with the most points wins the hunt. However, they must be careful, because there is a five-point deduction if they are running, being loud, or causing a disruption in the mall. So warn everyone to be on his or her best behavior.

3-Point Items to Search For:
- Old hanger
- 3 business cards
- Blank price tag
- Plain "thank you" shopping bag
- Napkin with restaurant name from food court
- Employment application

5-Point Items to Search For:
- Shopping bag with store name
- Credit application
- Brochure
- Mall map
- Catalog
- Paper with every employee's signature in one store
- Picture of your team posing with a mannequin

10-Point Items to Search For:
- Sample of store product
- Nametag
- Something broken the store no longer needed
- "Open" or "Closed" sign
- Free food voucher
- Getting someone to say your name over the public address system

Bonuses:
- 20 points if you find a business card of a person with the same name as you
- 15 points if you can get someone to give you a picture of him- or herself
- 10 points if you receive free food from the food court

Picture Hunt

8 or more players

What You Need

❍ Paper and pen or computer with printer (to print lists)

This hunt involves using cameras, so the fact that most teens today have phones with cameras comes in handy. Separate the teens into teams of at least four players each. Give each team a list of things they must take pictures of to earn points. Each picture is given a point value based on how complicated it is to get the photo. Just assign the points according to what you feel would be the difficulty of achieving the photo based on your location. Here are some ideas:

- Someone dressed as a superhero
- Someone (who is not on the team) dancing
- A person dressed as an animal
- An empty coffee cup
- A team member proposing to a stranger
- Squirrel with a nut
- Half the team members in the air, and the other half with their feet planted
- A piece of art outside
- A child with a stuffed animal
- A group of people (not on the team) hugging
- A man with a purse
- Laundry in a dryer

Educational/Classroom Hunts

Sometimes when you are teaching children, things can become a little repetitive. Remember that there are always ways to keep them excited about learning—for example, a classroom hunt. The following hunts were developed to help children understand the importance of working toward a goal and observing their surroundings.

Kindergarten Hunt

Since kindergarteners are learning all about shapes, colors, numbers, and letters in school, what better way to teach than to do a hunt using the things that surround them each day along with the things they are learning about in class? Here is a list to get things started. Some of the children may need help, but this game makes learning fun!

Colors
- Blue
- Red
- Yellow
- Green
- Purple
- Black
- White
- Orange
- Pink
- Brown

Shapes
- Square
- Round
- Oval
- Star
- Diamond
- Rectangle

Numbers

Find each number from 0 through 9.

Letters

You can hunt for each letter in the alphabet, or concentrate on upper-case and lowercase.

Classroom Supply Hunt

Elementary-to-middle-school ages

When children are in school all day, sometimes it's nice for them to take a break and play a game. It's also nice when the game can teach children to work with those around them and to use some cognitive thinking.

Here is a list of items that are commonly found in a classroom: hand sanitizer, glue, scissors, pencil sharpener, tissues, monthly calendar, crayons, paper, assignment list, computer, teacher workbook, list of classroom rules, bathroom key, and a tardy slip. It is best to number the items so that they have to check off that they found them and verify it by including the number written on it.

QUESTION

I homeschool my children. Are there educational hunts available?
Yes! With a little bit of tweaking, any of these hunts can be used in the home for educational purposes. Make sure to consider the space that you have available, what exactly you are trying to teach, and the age of the child or children participating.

Getting-to-Know-You Classroom Hunt

This hunt is especially helpful when you want your students to get to know one another. The students are all to be given the same list for the hunt. They are then asked to go around to each of their peers to find out who has what related to the list. They must then write down the name of the person next to the item that pertains to him or her.

For example, if one of the items on the list says "someone who likes funny movies," players will need to ask their peers if they like funny movies. Once they find someone who does like funny movies, they can write his or her name next to the item on the list. Here are some examples to get the kids started:

Someone who . . . skates, has blue eyes, has green eyes, has brown eyes, can swim, has been on an airplane, has lived in a foreign country, likes scary movies, says science is his or her favorite subject, plays a sport, rides the bus home, has a cat, has more than one dog, has been to Disney Land, has swum in the ocean, likes snow, has never eaten carrots, doesn't like chocolate, or plays an instrument.

Coded Hunts

Creating a secret code for a scavenger hunt can be easy, but it can also be time-consuming. The key is to make sure it all links up and leads to a final clue. The following secret code is simple, using letters in each clue to lead to a final message revealing where the prize is. This is an example, as locations obviously change per situation, but it is a start:

1. The second letter in a Hawaiian greeting _ _ _ _ _ = L from Aloha
2. Second letter in not the father, the _ _ _ _ _ _ = O from Mother
3. Third or last letter in another word for picture _ _ _ _ _ = O from Photo
4. The first letter in married to the queen _ _ _ _ = K from King
5. First letter in opposite of down _ _ = U from Up
6. First letter in gift, also known as a _ _ _ _ _ _ _ = P from Present

In this instance, all the letters spell out "Look up," so you could hide the prize up somewhere high.

Another way to do coding is to use numbers in place of letters, and only give away certain numbers and letters to get them started. Like this:

Hints: E=4 and 12=S

4 13 4 6 17 23 18 4   2 23 13 4 12   1 23   4 11 1
16 11 22 4   11 18 9 5 16 4   5 6 4 11 20.   12 23

14 2 4 11 12 4   7 23 5 18   15 12   5 18   1 3 4   22 5 1 16 3 4 18.

Solved, it reads:

Everyone loves to eat cake and ice cream. So please join us in the kitchen.

Another great way to use secret code is to come up with a list of pictures, and assign a letter to each photo. For example:

a = ■   b = ✖   c = ◆   d = ●   e = ♥   f = ◗   g = ✪   h = ▲

You can use any symbols or photos to stand for the letters. It takes some patience for the initial preparation of the code, but once you have it down, completing your hunt becomes much easier.

Are there any resources available to help create codes or assist in coded hunts?
There are several websites available that you can find by using your search engine. Some of the sites have initial fees for using the codes and having them personalized, while other sites have them already made and you can alter them as you like.

Map Hunts

There are several factors to consider when developing a map-based scavenger hunt. You need to think about the age group, the location, the theme (if there is one), and what treats or prizes will serve as the treasure at the end. If you are working with smaller children, it is usually best to use pictures or drawings as your clues. If the children are at an age where they have good comprehension skills, you can use several methods to develop your clues along the way.

For example, for each location on the map, they might find a puzzle piece, people, landmarks, or written riddles that get more complicated with each step. Put an X on the map as an end point, and provide written clues at each location, like, "Take 13 paces forward and hop over the big rock." The players use the map as a way to find the location of the next clue, but it also forces them to think about where it is within the general area, based on the clues. Here are some examples of maps for scavenger hunts.

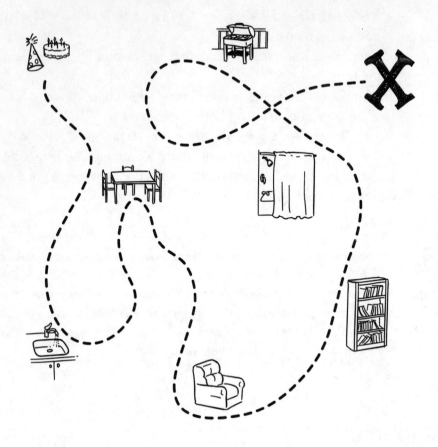

MAP FOR YOUNG CHILDREN

This type of map helps kids find where the clues are by using pictures that relate to rooms or furniture in the house, outdoor areas, etc. The example shown here starts in the party area and goes on to the kitchen, then the dining room, living room, bedroom, bathroom, outside, and then to the treasure.

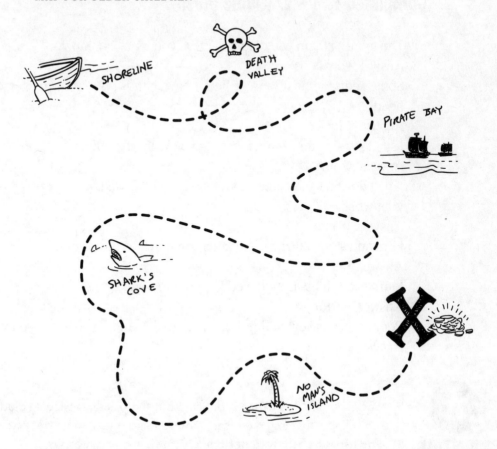

This type of map focuses more on the clues than actual representations of places. For the example shown here, older children are aware they are not really on an island, but they can pretend and use the written clues to guide them to each location.

Rhyme and Reason Hunts

Hunts that are based on rhyme and reason clues can be a great amount of fun. Trying to figure out a riddle or complete a rhyme is a wonderful way to engage a child's problem-solving skills. You can either start with a complete rhyme, guiding the players to a place or another clue, or use hinting riddles that set it up so that the answer completes the rhyme. Here are some examples that can be used in a scavenger hunt.

Completed Rhyme/Riddle Clues

The more of them you take, the more you leave behind you.
Answer: Footsteps
Some keep me next to their bed; I have hands with no arms, a face yet no head.
Answer: Clock
I shed my skin and I won't cry, but you will; what am I?
Answer: Onion
If you don't have me, then parties might be missed, and I'm usually worn on your wrist.
Answer: Watch
Firm and stout, I turn about, keep some in and others out.
Answer: Key
I turn everything around, yet I do not move.
Answer: Mirror
Poor people have it and rich people need it, and if you eat it, you will die.
Answer: Nothing

ESSENTIAL

Some people find rhyming difficult, but there is an available solution. It's called a rhyming dictionary. You can find one in most bookstores and use it to help with designing your rhyme and reasons.

Directional Clues

Go to the room used to prepare and heat, lots of yummy things to eat.
Answer: Kitchen
After a day with all you have seen, go to this room to get soapy clean.
Answer: Bathroom
From top to bottom, bottom to top, you climb me each day, and that won't soon stop.
Answer: Stairs
On top you sleep, and lay your head, but the thing you seek is under instead.

Answer: Bed

To be used I must break, and then I can be fried, poached, or baked.

Answer: Egg

I never fall up, I can only fall down, and people love to listen to my rhythmic sound.

Answer: Rain

If I eat I am fine, if I drink I die, your pants will catch me if you tell a lie.

Answer: Fire

Incomplete Rhyme Clues

I can grow fruits, flowers, and nuts you see, I change with each season, look for a . . .

Answer: Tree

You lie right here to rest your head, I come in all sizes, I am a . . .

Answer: Bed

A day without rest can make you a grouch, some people rest atop me, for I am a . . .

Answer: Couch

We're higher than clouds, buildings, and cars, shining so bright, we are the . . .

Answer: Stars

People do stare when they see me, playing shows and games I am the . . .

Answer: TV

Wind is my enemy, and water I can't handle, I burn for hours, look for a . . .

Answer: Candle

I can be caught but your hands cannot hold, to throw me or touch me, because I am a . . .

Answer: Cold

Car Trip Hunts

Whether it is a two-hour car trip or an eighteen-hour ride, sitting in a car can cause anyone to become restless. That is why the best thing anyone can do is to prepare for the trip with a variety of games.

Déjà Vu

What You Need

○ Index cards
○ Writing utensils

When the trip begins, you should hand the index cards and writing utensils to the restless riders. They are to write down or draw pictures of things that they see throughout the trip. This hunt can be played a couple of ways. If it is a one-way trip, halfway through they can switch cards with another passenger and try to locate each item.

If there isn't another passenger, the person can attempt to find the things again. If there will be a trip back, then they can use the cards on the way back to try to find the same things. You can also laminate the cards so they can be used for future trips.

FACT

The repetitive motion of a vehicle disturbs the inner ear's equilibrium and causes motion sickness. A good way to avoid carsickness is to look out the window and keep your eyes focused on something outside of the car.

Traveling Seek-and-Find

What You Need

○ Poster board (which won't easily tear)
○ Markers

Another way to prepare for a road trip is to come up with a checklist of items for the child or children to find. If you are not too crazy about using poster board and markers to create the checklist, you can always use an iPad or Nook to create a document the children can pull up and check off as you drive. But for those that want to keep it homemade, all you have to do is cut the poster board to a size suitable for the child to hold.

Here are some things commonly and uncommonly seen on a road trip that would work great on a car scavenger hunt: a bus, railroad tracks, a yellow flashing light, a church, a playground, a motorcycle, a semi truck, a license plate with an X in it, a purple car, a school bus, a silo, a restaurant billboard, a train in motion, cows, farm equipment, deer, a road construction sign, a police officer giving a ticket, a limo, a Hawaii license plate, an airplane, and a body of water.

CHAPTER 7

Minute-to-Win Games

Minute-to-win games have become overwhelmingly popular ever since the debut of the *Minute to Win It* television show. Since this chapter is broken up into age groups and categories, it will be easier for you to find activities appropriate for your specific party. All you have to do is accept the challenge and play!

Minute-to-Win Preschoolers

You're never too young to have fun with a one-minute challenge! These games are designed specifically for preschool-aged children so that they can compete just like the older players.

The Rattle

What You Need

- ○ 2 empty plastic 2-liter bottles
- ○ Duct tape
- ○ Gumballs, about 100
- ○ Stopwatch

Put the gumballs into one of the bottles and sit it on a flat surface. Take the empty bottle and put it opening to opening with the other bottle and tape them together. Make sure to tape them together well so that they do not come apart while being shaken. Set the stopwatch for one minute. The child must then shake the gumballs from one side of the bottles to the other before time is up. Tell him or her to keep shaking so that the center doesn't become clogged.

ALERT

When playing The Rattle, allow for extra room, and make sure that the players are extra careful when swinging the two-liter bottle around so that no one is at risk of being hit. Also, make sure that the gumballs are in a safe place, because they are a choking hazard.

Heads Up

What You Need

- ○ Balloons
- ○ Stopwatch

Have the preschoolers gather around to watch an adult do this one first so they can see what it is you mean when explaining the game. Inflate a balloon with air. The object of the game is to keep the balloon in the air for one minute, but you can only use your head—no hands. If the tots have a hard time, you can let them use their hands. Every child is different, so changing it up a bit won't hurt a thing.

Cookie Face

What You Need

○ Cookies
○ Stopwatch

Give the players a cookie and tell them that they must keep the cookie on their face while they walk in a straight line. The cookie should be placed on the forehead, and once time starts, the preschoolers have to walk across a yard or room without it falling off.

Color Blow

What You Need

○ 7 Ping-Pong balls (2 need to be a different color)
○ Cutting board (handheld)
○ Stopwatch

Place the balls on the cutting board, keeping the two that are colored in the middle. When the clock starts, the player will have one minute to blow all of the balls off the cutting board. The catch is that they have to leave the two balls that are a different color on the board.

Minute-to-Win Kids

These minute-to-win games are a great time for all ages. All you need are willing participants!

Dicey

What You Need

○ Popsicle sticks
○ Playing dice
○ Stopwatch

This takes some concentration and lip power. The player must put a Popsicle stick in his or her mouth and then stack five dice on the end of the stick without any of them falling off. The dice cannot rest against any part of his or her face. If the dice fall off, the child can start over, but the clock keeps going. The child wins if this is accomplished in a minute or less.

Blown Away

What You Need

○ Plastic cups
○ Balloons
○ Stopwatch

Line up five plastic cups on a table and hand the player a balloon. When the clock starts, the child has to blow the balloon up, release the air toward the cups, and try to knock the cups off the table. The child can blow the balloon up as much or as little as he or she wants. If the child is successful, he or she wins the challenge and a prize.

Chocolate Unicorn

What You Need

○ 6 chocolate snack cakes (like Hostess Ding Dongs)
○ Stopwatch

Anytime you have snacks involved in a game, almost everyone is willing to play. The object of the game is for the children to stack six of the snack cakes on their forehead, one on top of another. This needs to be finished within the sixty seconds so that you can see if the stack will hold for a minimum of three seconds. If it's accomplished, they win.

Chop Stack

What You Need

○ Chopsticks
○ 4 tubes of lip balm
○ Stopwatch

The object of this game is to use the chopsticks to stack all four tubes of lip balm (lengthwise), one on top the other without them falling over. Make sure the lids on the lip balms are completely flat and not rounded or this will not work. The stack must stay up for three seconds, before the one-minute time limit is up.

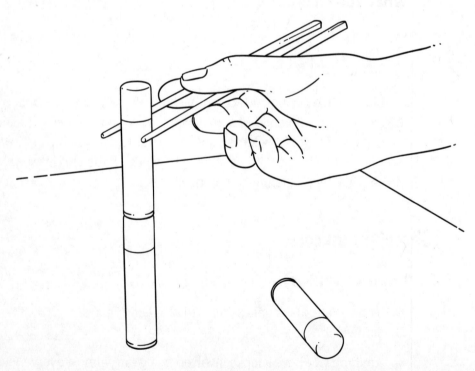

Minute-to-Win Tweens

These games are centered on speed and coordination, which is great for any tween. They cause them to focus to get the deed done before that minute mark is up.

Mini Cup Pyramid

What You Need

○ A package of (5-ounce) paper cups
○ Stopwatch

Have a sleeve of five-ounce paper cups laid out on a table. When the clock starts, the player must start a stack of cups totaling forty-five cups. The bottom row will be nine cups, and then a row of eight, followed by a row of seven, and so on, until the top of the pyramid is one cup. If it falls over, the player can start again but will still have to complete it before the minute is up.

Noodling Around

What You Need

○ Dry spaghetti noodles
○ Dry penne pasta
○ Stopwatch

Start this one by placing the penne pasta on the table. At the start of the game, the players must stand with their hands beside them. On "Go," the players will grab a piece of spaghetti and put it in their mouth. They now have to pick up six pieces of the penne pasta with the spaghetti noodle. The penne cannot enter their mouth, and if the spaghetti noodle breaks, they can continue to play only if it is still long enough to gather all six pieces. If it is too small, they are disqualified. If a penne drops off the noodle, it can still be used if it lands on the table. If it bounces off, the player is disqualified. Of course, the rules can always be altered to suit those playing.

Head Pendulum

What You Need

- ○ Baseball
- ○ Pair of pantyhose
- ○ 6 empty water bottles
- ○ Stopwatch

This game seems very simple, but it takes patience and concentration. First line up the bottles, spreading them out in a circle. Have the person who is playing stand in the middle. He or she will need to put the baseball in the bottom of one leg of the pantyhose. He or she will then need to slide the waist of the pantyhose over his or her head and tie it tight with the empty leg of the hose.

Once the pantyhose are secure, the player will place his or her hands behind the back and try to knock down all of the bottles without any use of the hands or feet, swinging the ball in the hose like a pendulum. If the player knocks them down in a minute or less, he or she wins the challenge.

ESSENTIAL

You can replace the items in this game with what is available in the house. The baseball can be any round, heavy fruit, while the pantyhose can be leggings tied at the end. For shorter players, you can use children's tights in place of pantyhose.

Bobble Head

What You Need

- ○ Pedometer clamped to a headband
- ○ Stopwatch

This game is a dizzy one. You have to strap the pedometer headband onto your head and make sure that it is set to zero. When the timer starts, you will need to move your head and body to get the pedometer to start registering steps. If the headband starts to slip off you can fix it, but keep going. If you reach 125 steps in one minute, you win this game.

Minute-to-Win Teens

Minute-to-win games are a popular party theme for teens. Here are a few of the games suitable for teenagers to play.

Breakfast Scramble

What You Need

- ○ Front of a cereal box
- ○ Scissors
- ○ Tape
- ○ Stopwatch

Before the game starts, you will need to cut the front of the cereal box into sixteen same-size pieces and mix them up. The object of this game is to put all the pieces back in order and tape them up in under a minute.

Shakedown

What You Need

- ○ Empty tissue box
- ○ Bag of bouncy balls
- ○ String
- ○ Tape
- ○ Stopwatch

You will need to prepare the tissue box so that it will go around your waist. Tape a string securely around the tissue box. Fill the box with bouncy balls and tie the box around your waist like a belt. When the minute starts, you will need to shake your body as much as possible to get all of the balls to fall out of the tissue box. If you are successful, you win the game.

Increase the laughter that this game brings by adding some background music. It will also help the person shaking like crazy to move a little better with a beat going. Anything that has a fast beat and gets the player moving will work just fine.

Tweezed

What You Need

- ❍ Tweezers
- ❍ Tennis racket
- ❍ Cup
- ❍ Tic Tac mints
- ❍ Stopwatch

If you liked playing the game Operation (originally made by Milton Bradley, now by Hasbro) as a child, you will like this game as an adult. A tennis racket is laid on a table. You will need to balance a tennis ball on the head of the racket and place a cup on one side of the racket.

You are given a pair of tweezers and must pick up a Tic Tac and put it through one of the holes and drop it into the cup. You cannot move the racket or touch it with your hands. If the Tic Tac doesn't make it into the cup you can try again, but if the ball falls off or the racket falls, the game is over. If you can get the Tic Tac in the cup before one minute is up, you win.

Caddy Stack

What You Need

- ❍ 3 golf balls
- ❍ Stopwatch

Place the three golf balls on a flat surface. When the clock starts, you will have to stack the golf balls, one on top of the other. If you can get all three of the balls stacked and staying that way for at least three seconds, you win.

Minute-to-Win Adults

Getting together as adults usually consists of conversation and dining together. As people get older, they tend to forget the joys of a good challenge. Minute-to-win games for adults help everyone get wrapped up in play and good fun.

Stack 'em High

What You Need

- ○ 36 plastic cups
- ○ Stopwatch

With this game there is little room for mistakes, so try and be as careful as you can. With one minute on the clock, the player must take the stack of thirty-six cups and build a pyramid, starting with a bottom row of eight cups and leading up to one cup at the top. The player must then put the cups back into a single stack before time is up. If he or she can complete the task, they win.

FACT

The NBC television show *Minute to Win It*, originally hosted by Guy Fieri, has had a very popular run. Many people don't know that he is also a chef that hosts a traveling cooking show called *Diners, Drive-Ins, and Dives*. He travels around trying different foods at locally famous food hot-spots.

Drop, Sink, and Clink

What You Need

- ○ Water
- ○ 3 (2-gallon) fish bowls
- ○ 3 shot glasses

○ A cup of quarters
○ Stopwatch

Fill the fishbowls up about 75 percent of the way and put a shot glass in the middle of each one, then place the fishbowls on the floor in a row. When the clock starts, you will need to grab one quarter at a time and drop it into the shot glass inside of the bowl. You must drop the quarter from three feet up. If you can make the quarter into all three shot glasses, you win the game.

Floatacious

What You Need

○ Bowl of water
○ Plastic plate
○ 5 empty aluminum cans with tabs removed
○ Stopwatch

This is definitely one of the harder games, but it can be conquered with a little patience. Fill the bowl of water up to almost full. Place the plastic plate on one side of the bowl and the cans on the other side of the bowl. When the timer starts, you have to put the plate on the water and begin stacking the cans, one on top of the other. If you get them all stacked up and they stay stacked for at least three seconds, you have won this challenge.

Yank Me

What You Need

- ○ 5 plastic cups
- ○ 4 index cards
- ○ Stopwatch

The objective of this game is to return the cups, turned upside down, into a nested stack. When the clock starts, you will take the upside-down cups and stack them one by one, placing an index card in between each layer. Once they are set up you must remove the index cards, starting with the top one. Once all the cups are nested back in a stack you are done. You win this challenge only if you can get it all done before the minute is up and by not dropping any of the cups.

Minute-to-Win Family

Playing minute-to-win games as a family can be a great way to bond with one another. Everyone taking a turn at solving a challenge makes for healthy competition. Plus players can also help one another with pointers and practice team-working skills.

Volcano

What You Need

- ○ 2-liter bottle of soda
- ○ Mints
- ○ Stopwatch

This one is fun for the entire family because it also is a bit of a science experiment. You will need to kneel on a chair or any elevated surface. Place the two-liter bottle below you and hold the mints in your hand. If you can get a mint into the soda in less than a minute and cause a volcanic eruption, you win!

ESSENTIAL

Playing minute-to-win games as a family gives you great opportunities to take memorable pictures and videos. These photos can be used for Christmas cards or your next family portrait.

Uphill Battle

What You Need

- ○ Marbles
- ○ 2 phonebooks or thick books
- ○ Wooden spoon
- ○ Stopwatch

To get this game ready, you will need to place the books under two of the legs of a table, giving the table a minor slant. Gather three of the marbles onto the spoon and hold them to the table. When the timer starts, you will let the marbles go and keep them from going off the table by tapping them with the spoon. You can only use one hand to hold the spoon, and no other part of you is to make contact with anything. If you can keep the marbles from rolling off for one minute, you win the game.

Leap Spoon

What You Need

- ○ 6 spoons
- ○ 3 glasses
- ○ Stopwatch

For this game, you will need to line up three glasses in a row. Lay the spoons on the table. When the timer starts you will begin flipping the spoons, in a single motion, by hitting the ends. You are trying to flip one into each glass. The spoons must touch the bottom of the inside of the glasses for them to count. If you can complete this before time is up, you win.

Tea Party

What You Need

- ○ Tea bags
- ○ Baseball cap
- ○ Duct tape
- ○ Stopwatch

Start by taping the tea bag strings to the bill of the hat, one on each side. Put the hat on and set the stopwatch for one minute. When the clock starts, you will need to swing your head in an attempt to get the tea bags to land on the top of the bill. They must stay on top of the bill for three seconds. If you complete this task, you win the challenge.

Minute-to-Win Office

Whether it is an office party or just another day at work, if you have downtime at your place of employment, you can play a couple of these games. You can even set it up so that those who accept and complete the challenges get to delegate simple tasks for other workers who fail to win their challenges.

Office Fling

What You Need

- ○ Chair with four legs
- ○ Large rubber bands

○ Stopwatch

This game is a great way to use up some free time at work. Take a chair and flip it upside down. Run a rubber band around two of the legs to act as a slingshot, and use wadded-up paper for your launching items. The object of the game is to get one of the paper wads to land on a desk and stay on the desk.

Clipboard Tennis

What You Need

○ Clipboard
○ Trashcan
○ Stopwatch

Wad up some paper balls, and stand about fifteen feet from a wastebasket. Have a coworker toss some paper wads at you, while you use the clipboard to hit them into the trashcan. You must get two in before the one-minute mark is up.

ALERT

Before playing these games at work, you may want to check with your human resources department to make sure that it is okay, just to cover all grounds and to refrain from any legal issues arising.

Office Fishing

What You Need

○ Pencil
○ String
○ Paper clip
○ Keys
○ Stopwatch

Begin this game by tying a string to the end of a pencil. At the end of the string you will attach a paper clip that has been unfolded and pinched into the shape of a hook. Sit a set of keys on the floor. You now have one minute to fish the keys up from the floor using your office fishing rod.

Paper Scraper

What You Need

○ 30 index cards
○ Stopwatch

With this neat little office game, you will use index cards to build a ten-story "paper scraper." Fold all but ten of the index cards in half. When the minute countdown starts, you will begin by placing two of the bent cards on the table side by side. Top these with a flat index card and then two more of the bent cards. Once you have gotten ten stories high and it stays intact for at least three seconds, you win the game.

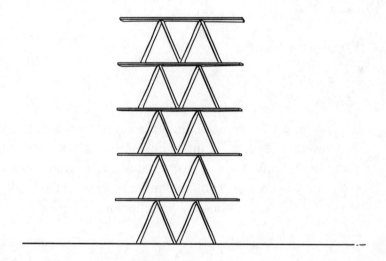

Minute-to-Win Holiday

A game can be a great addition to any holiday party. Whether it is a festive celebration at home or in the office with the coworkers, a minute-to-win game will bring some holiday cheer to any get together. Be sure to keep an eye on the clock though!

Mummy Wrap

What You Need

- ◯ 1 roll of toilet paper
- ◯ Holder to keep the toilet paper stable
- ◯ Stopwatch

This is a great Halloween minute-to-win game. With the toilet paper on a holder, grab one sheet. When the clock starts you will start spinning in circles, wrapping yourself like a mummy. If the toilet paper breaks at any time, the game is over. If you can wrap yourself in the entire roll, with no breaks in the tissue, in under a minute, you are the mummy-challenge winner.

Turkey Blow

What You Need

- ◯ Turkey feather
- ◯ Stopwatch

For this game, you must throw the feather in the air when the timer starts. You have to keep it in the air by blowing on it. You cannot touch it with any part of your body. If it hits the ground or lands on something before the minute is up, you are out. If you can manage to keep the feather in the air, then you deserve the wishbone for winning this challenge.

QUESTION

Where can you find a turkey feather?
Depending on where you live, some stores offer turkey feathers, but if they are not readily available, there is no reason to panic. You can always use a regular large feather in place of the turkey feather; surely most people won't even notice.

Christmas in the Balance

2 players

What You Need

○ Wrapping-paper tube
○ Yardstick
○ 10 ornaments on hooks
○ Stopwatch

Begin by placing the wrapping-paper tube in a standing, upright position. Balance the yardstick flat on top of the tube, then start the clock. Each player must place one ornament on each end of the yardstick without touching the stick or tube, and can only place one ornament on at a time per person.

After making sure each pair of ornaments are stable, the team can then move on to the next two ornaments, repeating the same process. If anything falls off or apart, the game is over. If your team gets all the ornaments on, and the whole thing stands for three seconds, you win the challenge.

Candy Cane Fishing

What You Need

- ⭘ Regular-size candy canes
- ⭘ String
- ⭘ Mini candy canes

Tie a string around the long end of the candy cane where the hook is hanging. Open ten of the mini candy canes and place them, hook side out, on the edge of a table. The object of this game is to fish for the mini candy canes with the big candy cane. Put the string in your mouth and let the candy cane hang. Now, pick up five of the mini candy canes, and keep them on the hook before the minute is up.

CHAPTER 8

Art and Creativity Games

Getting creative comes naturally to some, but not everyone. Sometimes, it takes a bit of guidance and help to get the creative juices flowing. Playing a game can help. Just remember, there is no such thing as being "good" or "bad" at art. Everyone expresses himself or herself differently. As an added bonus, guests can take the art pieces they create at your party home as party favors. The following games and activities will have everyone trying out a bit of his or her own artsy ways.

Painting Games

Paint is used as a way to express one's self artistically. Nothing that you paint even has to make sense. All that matters is that you enjoy yourself while you are painting. Invite your guests to let their creative juices flow and indulge in some artistic playfulness. Here are some ideas for using paint as a party game or activity.

Artist's Paint-and-Pass

4 or more players

What You Need

- ○ Paints
- ○ Brushes
- ○ Large piece of paper

Have everyone gather around a table. Place one sheet of paper in front of one of the painters and put the paints in the middle of the table with the brushes. Artists will paint whatever they like for one minute on the paper and then pass it to the left. The paper will continue around the table until everyone has a turn.

QUESTION

What types of paint should I use for these games?
You can use craft paint, acrylic, oil, or finger paints. There are a wide variety of paints available in art departments of most stores. It should be based on age and what you may have to clean up after all is said and done.

Brush, Brush, Paint

6 or more players

What You Need

❍ Paints
❍ Paintbrushes
❍ Large sheet of paper

This game is the artist's version of Duck, Duck, Goose. Have all the players gather around in a circle. Hang the large sheet of paper on a wall or a large flat surface. Put the paintbrushes in the middle and choose one person to begin the game. This person will grab a paintbrush and begin walking on the outside of the circle of people. As the person walks around, he or she will tap people, saying "brush, brush," and when someone is chosen, he or she will say "paint."

This person will stand up and take the paintbrush and paint on the paper for one minute. He or she will then grab a fresh brush and do as the first player did, circling the people, saying "brush, brush, paint." This can be played as long as you like or until you feel the painting is complete.

FACT

Did you know that the famous painter Pablo Picasso painted his first picture when he was just nine years old? Called *Le Picador*, it is a painting of a man on a horse during a bullfight. He was fifteen when he completed his first successful painting, called *First Communion*, which showed his family on the altar of a church.

Blow Painting

2 or more players

What You Need

❍ Paints
❍ Party blowouts
❍ Several medium pieces of paper

Painting doesn't always have to be done with paintbrushes. Changing up the traditional way of doing things is what art is all about. This activity is usually best when done outside because it can be a bit messy; however, with a couple of newspapers on the floor, it can be done in the house.

Hang up each paper on a wall and give each painter a blowout, and place paints in the center. To begin, the painters will dip their blowouts in paint. They will then blow them at the paper. This makes some very neat splash art the painters can take home with they are done.

Photography Games

Using cameras helps people to capture moments in an instant. While most do their best to remember each moment the best they can, it is always much easier to just snap a photo. Using photography as a party game or activity helps to collect memories without too much effort.

Photo Memory

What You Need

○ Photos of common objects
○ Objects from photos

It's best to prepare for this game ahead of time. Using household items, set up a photo shoot. You can stack fruit in a bowl or place toys on a table— anything you feel could be replicated by your target age group. You will get the photos developed and have them ready for the party, along with the pieces used in the photo shoot.

You will then ask the guests to gather around in a circle. They will take turns looking at a photo for twenty seconds and then using the pieces in front of them to try and recreate it from memory. They are all given different photos to look at. This way they are all working toward winning the game at the same time. The one (or ones) who is (or are) most accurate win(s) the game.

Framed

What You Need

- ❍ Empty picture frame (no glass)
- ❍ Wearable props (hats, scarves, glasses)
- ❍ Camera

This is a great photo opportunity for your gathering. Have your guests hold the empty frame up and strike a pose. You will take pictures of the guests acting silly and can print or download them later and distribute as late party favors. Looking back at a goofy photo can only make you laugh.

Many different cultures believed at one time that having your photograph taken would steal your soul. As the world has advanced, that belief has changed for most. Yet some Aborigines of Australia still refuse to have their photo taken because of this belief.

Mug Shots

What You Need

- ❍ Small dry erase board
- ❍ Dry erase markers
- ❍ Camera
- ❍ Photo printer

Uh oh, your guests have been busted! They are in trouble and have to have their mug shot taken. Create a mug-shot card using the board and markers. As your guests come up, put their name on the board and the reason they were arrested. This could be anything you can think of, but funny is always best. Once you are done with the photos, and if you have a printer on hand, you can print out their photos and send them home.

Dough and Clay Games

Playing with dough or clay is an inexpensive way to involve arts in game time. Playing with dough can keep people captivated for hours. If you were planning to have a younger crowd over, this would be perfect to keep them occupied.

Sculptor

What You Need

- ❍ Dough or clay
- ❍ Plastic butter knives
- ❍ Plastic play mats or plates

Have the sculptors sit in a circle and place their supplies in front of them. Tell them that they all have to use their items to build a look-alike for the person to their right. Once they have completed their sculpture, they will show it off to everyone. If you want to use this as one of the parting gifts, the sculptors can give their creations to the people that they modeled them after.

Archaeology Dough

2 or more players

What You Need

- ❍ Dough
- ❍ Items from outside and inside the house (e.g., leaves, rocks, toys, etc.)
- ❍ Brown paper bags
- ❍ Pens and paper

Put several items in each bag and make sure not to have duplicates. Hand each child a bag and some dough. The children will need to sit spread out so that no one can see what object they have in their bag. The object of this game is to make an impression in the dough using the items in the bag. After everyone is done, place the impressions on the table. The children will use their paper and pen to write down what they think each impression is. The child with the most correct is the winner.

ESSENTIAL

If you want to take a shot at making your very own dough or clay, there are many easy do-it-yourself recipes available online. If you use your search engine, you can find ways to color the dough and even have the kids help as part of the project.

Wacky Dough

What You Need

- ○ Dough
- ○ Latex balloons
- ○ Googly eyes (available at craft stores)
- ○ Yarn
- ○ Glue
- ○ Scissors

Start by rolling your dough into a worm-like shape. Open the mouth of the balloon, and slide the dough worm inside. Cut ten pieces of yarn, each four inches long. Tie the balloon around the center of all of the yarn—this will be hair. Glue on some eyes, and let it dry. The children now have a cool, squishy toy to play with, or to give to a parent as a stress reliever.

Drawing and Sketching Games

Sitting down to draw when you have never tried before can be overwhelming. That is why it is important to remember that these activities are more to help bring out the artist in people, no matter how good they are. Trying something new is going to be funny, fun, or both, and it can't hurt to try.

Negative Art

What You Need

- ○ Paper
- ○ Scissors
- ○ Crayons, markers

Before the artists arrive, cut out a different shape or shapes on each of the pieces of paper. When the children arrive, give each child one of the papers and some coloring utensils. They must draw around the hole on the paper but still make it part of the picture. The negative spaces enable the artist to make art around the spaces that still works. It's a great way to get the creative juices flowing.

Flipbook Frenzy

What You Need

- ○ Several sticky notepads (preferably one for each guest)
- ○ Black fine-point markers

This might bring some people back to their childhood. This game leaves room for creativity, a few good laughs, and fun for everyone. Pass out a sticky notepad and marker to each participant. Have each person draw a stick figure on the first page of the pad. Participants can draw a background too, but it is best to keep it simple. Then have them flip to the next sticky page, leaving the first page stuck to the pad.

On each page, participants should copy the drawing on the page before, only changing a small detail about the stick figure. For example, to create a kung fu flipbook story, make the figure's leg move slightly with each page until a kick has been created. It's ultimately up to the artist to decide what will come of his or her stick figure. When the guests are done with their books, they can pass them around to share all the stories. Those familiar with this process can start with any art they want, as long as it works when the pages are flipped.

Model Drawing

What You Need

○ Paper
○ Drawing utensils

Ever dreamed about being a model or perhaps the muse for someone else's creations? This game gives everyone a shot at modeling. Have the guests take turns being the model for others to try to draw. They can do serious poses or funny poses—it's up to them. Once they are done with their drawings, they can look at how everyone has a different perspective when it comes to seeing and art.

Masquerade

What You Need

○ Plain white paper mache masks
○ Pastels
○ Pastel fixative spray

Making a mask is a great way to express one's self. You can be anything behind that mask—a superhero, a bird, or even an alien. It becomes whatever your mind thinks up. Supply the participants with pastels and have the people color their masks to their liking. Once they are done, you will need to spray a coat of fixative spray over the masks to make sure the colors stay on and do not bleed. Once they are dry, let the people roam around wearing the masks and pretending to be whatever they like.

One-Man's-Trash Art Games

Buying art supplies can become a bit pricey if you have certain ideas in mind. The following games only really require items that people throw away. It helps to prepare a little by keeping some sturdy items to inspire others.

Can Lanterns

What You Need

- ○ Empty tin cans (no sharp edges)
- ○ Hammer
- ○ Several sizes of nails
- ○ Colored permanent markers
- ○ Votive candles
- ○ Towel

The night before the gathering, clean the cans out, fill with water, and place in the freezer (you will be hammering nails into them the next day, and this will make it much easier to do that). When you're ready to make your lanterns (you'll probably want to start this early, since they will need to thaw out), be sure that an adult performs the next step, with all children at a safe distance. Place each can on its side and hammer nails in, either using a design or just putting holes all over. Once you're finished, run the cans under hot water to get the ice to come out. Dry off the cans with the towel.

Using the markers, have everyone add color or pictures to the outside for decorations. If it's nighttime, have an adult light a votive candle inside each lantern. When the party is over, give each child one of the votive candles to take home with his or her lantern, making sure that parents are aware.

Box Guitar

What You Need

- ○ Empty rectangular tissue box
- ○ Rubber bands
- ○ Paper towel roll
- ○ Straw
- ○ Scissors
- ○ Tape
- ○ Paint and brushes (optional)

If you have decided to use paint, you will need to do this first so it can dry in time to make the guitar. Start by cutting a hole in one end of the box. Use the paper towel roll as a guide for size. Then cut six (1") slices at one end of the paper towel roll. This will keep it on the guitar.

From the center hole in the tissue box, run the tube up and out the hole you cut in the end. With the flaps folded up on the end of the tube it should stay secure; if you want to tape it to make sure, that is fine. Now wrap five rubber bands over the box, horizontally. Vertically run the straw underneath the rubber bands on the opposite end of the handle. Once this is done you should have a guitar. Now go play some tunes!

ESSENTIAL

These games are great to help explain the importance of recycling. Re-using the items that are commonly thrown away and pile up in landfills can establish how one man's trash can be another man's treasure, and reaffirm that beauty really is in the eye of the beholder.

Reshaped and Reused Crayons

What You Need

- ❍ Old, broken crayons without the paper
- ❍ Oven
- ❍ Old muffin tin, soap molds, or shaped candy molds
- ❍ Butter knife

Most people just throw crayons out when they break, but this is a great way to turn the trash into treasure. Preheat your oven to 250°F. Take all of the old, broken crayons and break them into 1" pieces or smaller. Place them in the molds until the molds are ¾ full. Bake them for ten to fifteen minutes, depending on the depth of the mold, remove, and let cool. Once they are cool, use your butter knife to help wedge them out. These are great take-home favors or parting gifts.

Food Art Games

Working with food doesn't always have to involve cooking it. Sometimes just seeing the potential art in what you eat can lead to fun activities and games. Try these out and have a little fun playing with your food for once.

Candy Wear

2 or more players

What You Need

- ○ Assorted candies with holes in them
- ○ String

This game doesn't have to be for girls just because it involves jewelry. The participants can use the string and candy to build necklaces, bracelets, nunchucks, or anything their creative little minds can come up with. Once they are done with their creations, players can show them off to one another, and eat them if they like!

Hungry Puzzler

What You Need

- ○ Assortment of cereal
- ○ Glue
- ○ 4" × 6" cards
- ○ Magazine page of people engaged in an activity (for example, playing sports or cooking)

First, cut the magazine page into sections and give each guest a piece of the picture. (Do not tell the guests what the larger picture shows.) Next, give each guest some cereal, glue, and a card and tell them to use the cereal to try and recreate the portion of the image they were given. Once everyone is done, gather all the cards together and try to figure out what the original picture was. You can split guests into groups and see who figures out the puzzle first. Whoever gets it right first is the winner!

ALERT

Before playing any of the games in this section, you should check with everyone to make sure there are no food allergies of any kind. Food allergies can cover a very large variety of foods. It is best to establish that you will be working with foods with the participants so that there are no surprises come game time.

Noodle City

4 or more players

What You Need

❍ Pasta of all shapes, colors, and sizes
❍ Liquid glue
❍ Paper plates
❍ Markers, glitter, and other art supplies

This is a group effort to build something all the players can be proud of. Each person will be given a paper plate and told that they are building a city together. The group can talk amongst themselves and decide what buildings or locations they want to build with their noodles and then begin. At the end of the gathering, when the noodle art has dried, they can view their Noodle City that they worked together to build.

Cupcake Wars

3 or more players

What You Need

❍ Cupcakes

○ Disposable cupcake tins
○ Sprinkles, sanding sugar, candies, icing

Everyone is a winner with this food game. Using the disposable muffin tins, you will use the cupcake toppings and fill each hole with a topping. Give the children a cupcake each—it's best to ice them right before you give them out; that way the decorations stick. They will have three minutes to decorate their cupcake the best they can. At the end you can give out prizes for most creative, most colorful, and any other category that would suit the cupcakes. You can even allow the prize to be that they get to eat their cupcake.

Blocks-and-Building Art Games

Watching something come together piece by piece can be very exciting for both the builder and the audience. Sometimes people don't realize just how capable they are of creating something great with simple blocks until they try. Here are some great building activities to bring the architect out in everyone.

Battle Kingdom

6 or more players

What You Need

○ Blocks, LEGOs, or foam building blocks
○ Gummy candies

This is a great little group competition. Have the players separate into groups. Give each group a set of building pieces and a bag of gummies. They will have fifteen minutes to work together and build a fort or kingdom. When the time is up, the war begins. Each team will launch an attack with the gummies. Whichever team does the most damage to the other team's kingdom becomes the winner.

FACT

Some of the largest LEGO structures in the world have been built by the LEGO Group itself. For example, in 2013, a life-size replica of the *Star Wars* movie ship the X-Wing Starfighter was built, which is said to be the largest LEGO model ever. It took more than 5.3 million LEGO bricks to build the entire thing. It stands at eleven feet tall, forty-three feet long, with a wingspan of forty-four feet wide, and has been displayed at LEGOLAND California.

Bridge Master

3 or more players

What You Need

- ○ LEGOs
- ○ Brown paper lunch bags
- ○ Eggs

This game can also act as a way to give out the party favors for the players. You will need to fill each bag with the matching pieces and amounts of LEGOs. Have the players sit away from each other so their pieces don't get mixed up and they don't copy one another. Instruct them that they have five minutes to use their pieces to build a sturdy bridge. After the five minutes is up, you will use the egg to test out whether the bridge can handle the weight of it. If the bridge stays intact with the egg on it, then they win a prize.

Skyscraper

3 or more players

What You Need

- ○ Blocks, LEGOs, or foam building blocks

This seems like a simple game, but if the partygoers like to build, they might enjoy making things more complicated! Set out the building pieces in the middle of a table. Have the children gather around and explain that the object of the game is to build the highest skyscraper without it crumbling or tipping over. The player that builds the highest skyscraper wins the game.

Team Memory

What You Need

○ Colored building blocks
○ Timer

This game requires a good memory and keen observation. Start by separating your guests into an even number of groups of three or more players per group. Each group will be given colored blocks and a team to compete against. Groups have two minutes to come up with a pattern using the colors of the blocks. To complicate things a little more for the other team/teams, each team will have five minutes to build something that incorporates their color pattern.

For example, a team could construct a building using the pattern of red, red, blue, green, green, red, and yellow. (Have the teams build out of sight of the others to eliminate any cheating.) Once the designs are complete, each team will be given two minutes to look at their competition's construction. When time is up, they have to rebuild it from memory. The design and pattern must be the same. If no teams can match their competition's building exactly, the team with the closest match wins the game.

CHAPTER 9

Office Party Games

Sometimes working in an office can become a bit mundane. A lot of the time people get so stuck in their routine that they don't even bother to break out of their shell and get to know their coworkers. These office games are sure to not only lighten the stress and atmosphere but to help everyone get to know one another.

Getting to Know Your Coworker

Sometimes getting to know a coworker can feel like a chore. It is hard to find a way to start a conversation with someone you barely know anything about. Having a good relationship with your coworkers is essential for a positive working environment. The following games should help ease the pain of introducing and getting to know your coworkers.

Nice to Meet You

This game is good to play when you have a staff that is unfamiliar with each other or for a new hire getting to know her or his new officemates. Have everyone sit in a circle. People are to ask the person to their left five questions about him- or herself. When the five minutes is up, have everyone go around and introduce that person to the group.

FACT

According to Benjamin Levy, the, author of *Remember Every Name Every Time*, you can remember anyone's name by using his FACE method. Focus on the person's face. Ask what he or she wants to be called, a nickname or such. Comment on the name, and link it to something you can remember it by, like a friend. For example, "Oh, I have another friend named Greg." Finally, use the person's name to say goodbye, and that it was nice to have met him or her.

Talent Search

Have all the employees gather around. One by one ask them if they have any special talents. It can be anything from origami, singing, being double-jointed—anything at all. Ask them to then showcase their talent for the next two to three minutes, based on what it is, of course.

Getting Together

For this game, you'll need someone to be the leader. Start off by getting everyone together in a common area. The object of the game is to name a category by which groups can be made. You could say, "Everyone gather in groups based on the state you were born in," or "Get into groups where everyone is wearing the same color." You may want to prepare your categories before you start the game. You can even include categories about the job in which you work—anything to get them feeling a sense of unity and common ground.

Nickname Nametag

What You Need

- ○ Nametags
- ○ Markers

This little game is sure to get participants laughing at themselves and others. As each guest arrives, give him or her a nametag and a marker. Guests should approach someone who is not already wearing a nametag and ask his or her name. They must then give that person a nickname, using the first letter of the person's name to choose the nickname. For example, nicknames could include Tough Tom, Loopy Leonard, Smart Sharon, or Excited Erica.

The person given the name can come up with a nickname for that person, or find another person to name. (Each person only nicknames one other guest, though.) Once the guests have a nametag, have them take a turn explaining whether their new nickname suits them or is far from the truth. This helps the group learn each others' names quickly and easily.

Team-Building Skills Games

Just because a group of people shares the same space every day doesn't mean they are working as a team. Most of the time, a workplace runs better when there is a strong feeling of teamwork and support. These games are ways to boost the team-building skills at work, so try some of these out.

Egg Drop

What You Need

○ Eggs

What better way to help with team-building skills than to give a group of people a challenge they need to solve together? First, separate the employees into groups. Each group will have to come up with a container that can (hopefully) hold the egg safely when dropped from six feet. When the groups are ready, they must present it to everyone and show how it works. The team with the most sensible container and best presentation wins.

Commercial Life

Have the staff split into several groups. They must pick any simple item from around the office and create a commercial for it. They will have fifteen minutes to get the commercial ready and then they will present it to the group. You can even give the groups index cards, and they can anonymously write down whether they would buy the product based on the commercial. The one with the most potential sales wins.

QUESTION

What are some good ways to get familiar with coworkers when you are a temporary hire?
If you are a temporary employee, you might find that most employees avoid getting to know you because they know you most likely won't stay. But playing a simple game of Twenty Questions at lunch can get everyone familiar with one another and make for a better work environment.

Sneak a Peak

What You Need

○ Children's building blocks

The leader of the group will need to build a structure from the blocks and place it somewhere no one can see it. Split the staff into teams and give each team a set of blocks. One person from each group will go over to where the structure is and observe it for fifteen seconds and then return to his or her group. The observer must describe it so that his or her team can build a replica with their blocks.

After two minutes of building, another team member from each group will go over and observe the structure for fifteen seconds. Then that person will return to his or her group and try to fix any mistakes to make it look the same as the original structure. This will continue until the groups have made a complete replica of the structure. First team to complete it wins.

Team Trivia

At least 3 teams of 2 or more people

What You Need

○ Index cards
○ Pens

○ Paper

This team-building game does require a bit of preparation, but is a great way to incorporate some competition and teamwork. Begin by making identical sets of trivia questions on the index cards—each team will need one.

The first category is country flags. Number one side of the index card from one to ten and write down the colors of the flags for ten different countries (write the colors in the order they appear on the flag, as best you can). On the other side of the card, write down the names of the ten different countries you are referring to, making sure they are not in the same order as the list on the front of the card. For example, you could write green, white, and orange on one side of the card, then write "Ireland" on the other side. The contestants will match the colors to the country.

Another category could be characters from popular movies or TV shows. For example, you could list Homer, Marge, Bart, Lisa, and Maggie on one side of the card. On the back, you could place multiple-choice options, such as the Cosbys, the Bradys, the Simpsons, etc. Feel free to come up with other categories as well.

Give each group a set of cards, paper, and a pen. When the game starts, the teams will work together to try to figure out as many trivia questions as possible. The team with the most correct answers wins the game.

Working Overtime Games

Few people really enjoy working overtime. Sometimes pay can keep workers motivated, but other times that is just not enough. This section has a couple of games you can play to get everyone feeling a little less stressed or overwhelmed.

Office Bowling

What You Need

○ 3 reams of paper
○ A grapefruit or large orange

Add a little life to your office! Set up three reams of paper side by side and have the players stand at least fifteen feet away from them. Hand the first player the "ball" to take a shot at knocking over all three reams at once. If this is accomplished, he or she will move on to the next round of taking a step back and starting again. Have the best players compete with one another to see who the office-bowling champ is.

Chair Race

What You Need

- ○ Rolling chairs
- ○ Toilet paper

You will need a wide hallway or open area for this one. Line up two chairs at one end of the race area. Use the toilet paper to set a finish line that players can break through at the end of the race. Have two employees start by sitting in the chairs. When the race starts, they should make their way to the finish line by using their feet and hands, but their bottoms cannot leave the seat during the race. The player to win the first round moves on to challenge the winner of the next race. This continues until there is a chair-racing victor.

FACT

The definition of stress is a state of emotion or mental strain resulting from adverse or very demanding situations. Stress can lead to health problems, including headaches, chest pains, insomnia, fatigue, and depression. That is why it is important to find ways to relieve stress—like playing games!

Office Ball

What You Need

- ○ Wadded-up paper

○ Several trashcans

Put the trashcans at several distances and heights, giving each one a point value. Employees will take turns to try to throw the wadded-up paper in the baskets. They can take as many shots as they want in two minutes. The points are then added up, and the employee with the highest score wins.

Games Incorporating Family

When your family visits your workplace, you want them to not only see where you work but to have an enjoyable experience as well. What better way to do this than to have the office and your family participate in a game together.

Family Exchange

What You Need

○ Pens
○ Paper
○ Bowl

This game can become very informative and quite entertaining for everyone involved. Give each person a pen and a piece of paper. Participants write down two things that describe them. For example, they could write, "I play basketball every weekend and waffles are my favorite food." They have to keep what they wrote a secret, fold it up, and place it in the bowl. Have the employees line up. One by one, they will pick a piece of paper, then go to the back of the line.

Everyone will continue to pick a piece of paper out of the bowl one at a time until the bowl is empty. The employees now read their slips of paper and try to figure out who is in their new "family." They can guess a name outright, or go around asking only yes-or-no questions to different people in the room. The person to figure out everyone in his or her new family first wins the game.

Flip-a-Song Karaoke

What You Need

○ iPod or CD player

Have everyone gather around the music device you have supplied. Ask for a volunteer to be the first singer. Allow the person to pick a song he or she knows, and set it up to play. Play the song for a moment so everyone can hear how it goes. Then cut the music off so that it is up to the singer to complete the next verse.

Here's the catch: The person must finish the song verse, but using a different genre of music. For example, if the person chose a rock song, he or she could finish the verse using a country twang. If it was a slow song, he or she could turn it into a rap. This game is great for office family time and lots of laughs.

ESSENTIAL

If you or someone in your family is always working late, it can be tough to find a lot of quality family time. Inviting your family into your work world somehow—by visiting at lunchtime, or having an older child spend a day in the office—can sometimes help them understand exactly what a day "at the office" really looks like. This, in turn, can bring you closer together.

Mad Lib Story

Large group

What You Need

○ Large board or paper to write on

Have the players gather around the board or paper. The leader asks the group to name ten random items, followed by ten random locations, and ten random people. Write it all down on the board.

Once the list is complete, the leader asks for a volunteer to start, revealing that it is a storytelling game. The player must choose one word from the list and make up five sentences in a story that each has the word incorporated into it. Then the next person then chooses a word and continues the story with five new sentences. The last person must wrap the story up. This game is good for laughs because everyone's creativity is so different!

Picture Match

What You Need

- ○ Pictures of employees when they were much younger
- ○ Index cards
- ○ Pens

Have each employee bring in a photo of him- or herself at a younger age. Make sure to secretly note somewhere which employee belongs with which photo. Hang each picture on a board and post the board up for everyone to see. The people who think they know who is who can use an index card to write down their answers. The employee or family member with the most correct answers wins.

Promotion Games

When someone has gotten promoted in your company, it is a good time to show how much you appreciate him or her. The following games should establish some good belly laughs as you thank the person for his or her hard work.

Blind Man's Treasure

What You Need

- ○ Small gifts to give away

Have everyone partner up. One of the partners is to be blindfolded. The host of the game will choose a gift, and once the players have their blindfold on, he or she will put it somewhere in the room. When the host says "Go," the blindfolded partners will be led to it by their seeing partners. The seeing partners cannot leave the spot they are in; they can only give verbal commands. You can do several rounds of this game or just one; it's really based on what time will permit.

ESSENTIAL

If you are given the task of planning a promotion party for someone you are unfamiliar with, things can get a bit hectic. Even if you are not very familiar with the person, doing a little footwork and asking questions can help you plan a great party for him or her. Find out things such as what foods the person likes, favorite hobbies, and music preference, and you'll have the basics you need to pull the party off!

Check Your Pockets

This game only requires someone to call out random objects to the group of guests. You can choose to have the guests separate into smaller groups and keep a point system. The caller will stand in front of the group/groups and call out a random item, like lipstick. The first person to run up with the item receives the points for it. The person or team with the most points at the end wins the game.

Following the Leader

What You Need

○ Bell or whistle

This game takes good observation skills. Start by gathering the guests into an area where everyone can hear you explain that when you ring the bell or blow the whistle, the participants must change something that they are doing.

For example, you could tell your guests that if you ring the bell, they must put down whatever is in their hands. The person or people to do it last is/are out of the game, or can take over as host. You can change what you want them to do every time you ring the bell or blow the whistle. The last one, or last few standing, is/are the winner(s).

Retirement Games

Retirements are farewells that are often hard to plan for. Saying goodbye to someone who has been around for a while can cause a party to turn into a sad moment. Retirement is supposed to be a joyous moment for the person who worked hard to get to where he or she is. Using games will get the party back to fun, and create some great parting memories.

I Remember

What You Need
- Index cards
- Pens
- Bowl

It really wouldn't be fair if the retiree got away with leaving and no one got to reminisce. Have the staff and guests of the party write down things about the retiree that stick out in their mind. They can be funny memories or moments they admired the person—anything they wish to share. Have them fold it up and place it in the bowl. Later in the party, have people go up one by one and read off the index cards. Seeing the retiree realize how much people remember about him or her should be fun to witness.

FACT

The average age for retirement in the United States is now 61 years old, meaning it has jumped up by four years since the early nineties. Having to work longer is all the more reason to throw a party for the retiree!

Prediction Bingo

What You Need

○ Blank bingo cards (printed out from the Internet, or you make them yourself)
○ Markers or pens
○ Prize (your choice)

Since this is a retirement party, most people are familiar with one another. When the guests arrive, hand them a blank bingo card and a marker. They must fill in the blank spaces on the card with their predictions for the evening.

For example, people can write what they think a particular person will say, that someone will fall asleep in the coatroom, or whatever they believe will happen during the party. After the guests have filled out a bingo card, they will mark the things off as they happen during the party. The person with the most correct predictions on his or her card at the end of the game wins Bingo.

B	I	N	G	O

Job Charades

What You Need

- ○ Index cards
- ○ Pens
- ○ Bowl

This is a twist on the classic game. Have all the guests grab an index card and write down a career or job. Suggest they think out of the box; that way, there will be fewer repeats with the cards. Have them drop them in a bowl, and one by one, have the guests come up and pull a card. They are now left with the task of acting out the career or job on the card. You can do a point system where the person with the most correct guesses wins or just have fun with it; it is, after all, a retirement party.

CHAPTER 10

Dinner Party Games

Hosting a dinner party is a great way to meet new people. There's really no need for a party theme or for rolling out the red carpet. Just turn on the oven, set the table, and you're good to go! The following games will help build new friendships and create great memories.

Couples' Games

A couples' dinner party is usually given as a way to take the night off from the kids or the daily grind of work. Either way, having a moment with your partner is always a great opportunity to reconnect. So kick back, relax, eat a little, and have a good laugh with your partner.

Soul Mate

What You Need

○ Paper
○ Pen

Before your guests arrive, you will need to write down a list of at least seven questions for the couples to answer. You can ask things like, "Where did we first meet?" "What is my favorite hobby?" "Who was my first kiss?" and anything that pertains to them and their relationship. When the game begins you will need to separate the partners and put them in different rooms. Go to one room, hand each person a pen and paper, and ask them the questions. They must write down their answers on the paper.

Once you are done you will have the couples reunite in the same room. You will then have one couple come up and stand or sit side by side. You will ask the question of the one partner, and after the response you will read the answer the partner gave. For each correctly answered question, the couple receives a point. The couple with the most points at the end of the game wins.

FACT

Have you ever heard the saying, "Couples that play together stay the together"? What better way to be with your partner than to be playing games and enjoying each other's company.

Switched

What You Need

○ Pen
○ Paper

Before your guests arrive, you will write down the name of each person attending the dinner on a piece of paper, one person per piece of paper. Have the seating laid out, and place the name of a person under each plate. As your guests finish up their dinner, they are to look under their plate and read the name to themselves. They are to now act like this person for the rest of the night.

The funny part is that they are to still be in a relationship with their own partner. With everyone acting as someone else, the relationship interactions should be quite funny. This will continue until the night ends. Have people write down who they think each person is, and the guest with the most correct wins the game.

Silly Bones

This couples' game is all about staying connected. Have your guests gather around, making sure they stand next to their partner. You will start with simple commands like, "The knee bone connects to the thighbone," or "The wrist bone connects with the neck bone." Each couple will have to keep the connections with one another for as long as possible. Continue the commands until there is only one couple left that is still connected at the areas mentioned by the host. The last couple connected wins the game.

Singles Games

Hosting a singles dinner is a great way for single people to gather and meet one another, partly because they know that they all have something in common: being single. Getting to know other singles by participating in a little goofy playtime can lead to good times and new friends.

The Message

What You Need

○ Pen
○ Scraps of paper

Before your guests arrive, write down several different goofy comments on the scraps of paper. Comments like, "I used to be a dog thief," "I eat cabbage every day," or something like "I have a pet worm." Anything will work, whether the comments are funny or just random. Place one piece of paper under each person's plate. When everyone has arrived, have each person take a seat and read his or her comment silently. Throughout the party, people will need to say their assigned comment during conversations with others. At the end of the night, everyone will gather around and try to guess who was joking about what.

Truth or Manners

During dinner your guests are to observe one another, looking for any behavior that is perceived as rude or inappropriate. Things like not putting a pinky up when drinking, not wiping your mouth with a napkin, putting elbows on the table, or answering a cell phone at the table. Any rules you establish in the beginning of the dinner will have to be adhered to during dinner. If someone is spotted doing something wrong, he or she is to be called out and asked a truth question. The person must then answer the question. The person who was asked the least amounts of questions at the end of dinner wins.

ESSENTIAL

You can always make your dinner party a little more interesting by testing your guests' knowledge of proper manners and etiquette. You can purchase a book of mannerisms at most bookstores and see just how much people know and remember throughout your dinner party.

All Thumbs

This game can go on during dinner and continue for the rest of the night if so desired. At the beginning of dinner, you will secretly assign someone to be the person who is all thumbs. This person will choose a time during dinner to place both of his her thumbs on the table, but not to say anything, and just wait for others to notice. When someone notices it, that person must place his or her thumbs on the table as well.

This continues until there is only one person who hasn't noticed. You can choose to have this person do something funny for losing, or reveal something special about the person, or just have him or her start the next round. This game will have your guests really trying to pay attention, and they are sure to laugh it up as it takes others a while to catch on.

Housewarming Games

Whether you are moving into a new house or you are throwing the house-warming bash for someone else, these parties are a great way to celebrate a new milestone. It is exciting moving into a new place and starting fresh. And hey, why not begin with a celebration? Because a little bit of conversation and a few interesting games can start your memory lane of home on the right path.

Room Recall

What You Need

- ○ Crayons
- ○ Paper

Take your guests to a room of your choice. Open the door, let them view the room for one minute, and let them know that must try to remember as much about the room as possible. Then close the door. Hand them each a piece of paper and some crayons, and have them recreate the room from memory.

This game is a little funnier if you have some truly random items laying around the room, like a stuffed cat, a bowl of socks, or anything that might strike someone as odd. The person to draw the room the most accurately wins the game. You can give bonus points for the odd items in the room if they are featured in their art.

The Grand Tour

This game is silly, and somewhat like the game known as Telephone. As the first guest arrives, give that person a tour of your home. As you go through the rooms, name something that you plan to do with the room, or to decorate it with. As the next guest arrives, the first guest will then give that person the tour, repeating each thing you said. The next guest will be given the tour by the previous guest, following the same rules.

Once the last tour has taken place, the final guest will take everyone on a tour, repeating what he or she was told. As you can imagine, hilarious things tend to come out as the guests struggle to remember what was actually said.

Homely Hunt

What You Need

○ Tape
○ Pictures of different homes
○ Marker
○ Small prizes

Before your guests arrive, you will need to number each picture of a home. For each number, assign a small gift as a reward for finding the home during the hunt. Tape the picture anywhere your guests will be at some point in the party. After all your guests have arrived, announce that there is a hunt in progress. Let them know that if they find pictures of homes, they win a prize. After all the pictures have been located, you can give out the prizes.

You can add a twist to the game by allowing the guests to keep or steal each other's gifts, going by number, like a dirty Santa or Yankee swap game. Assign each person a number (or have them pick numbers out of a hat) and the person with the lowest number can either choose to keep his or her gift or trade that gift for another. Each guest can only choose once. This continues until the person with the highest number is the last to keep or trade gifts with someone else.

After-Dinner Games

Now that everyone is stuffed and ready to relax, it's time to roll up your sleeves and get a little competitive.

Chicken Pox

What You Need

○ Round red stickers

As your guests finish up their dinner, hand each one a sheet of the red stickers. Explain to them that the rules of the game are that no one can call anyone by his or her real name. If you hear someone say someone's name, you are to put a red sticker on him or her. That person now has the chicken pox and can infect others by slyly encouraging them to say someone's name. By the end of the night, the person with the least amount of chicken pox wins the game.

Celebrity Dinner Theater

What You Need

○ Paper
○ Pen

Before your guests arrive, write down the names of several celebrities most people would be familiar with on a piece of paper. Place one name under each person's plate before everyone sits down to eat.

Once the guests are done eating, have them look under their plate and read the name silently. They now have to carry on like that celebrity, without acknowledging who they are, until someone can guess who they are. They can even act out some of the roles the celebrity has played or things the celebrity is famous for. This makes for ultra-interesting after-dinner conversations. The person to guess the most correct celebrities wins the game.

FACT

The word *dessert* comes from the French word *desservir*, which means to clear (away), or to serve. If you are looking for an easy desert, fudge is one of the simplest recipes to make. Telling yourself not to eat the entire pan is the hard part.

Ghost

There are no supplies needed for this game, but a good vocabulary will help. Choose a guest to be the first to pick a letter of the alphabet. The next person will choose another letter, and so on and so forth. The catch is that they are supposed to be spelling a word. You don't want to be the last letter, so you have to try to keep the word going.

For example, if you start with an M, then E, then L, you can do the word *melt*, and continue it into *melted*, *melting*, or any word you can extend from the base word. The last letter (person) becomes a "ghost" and exits the game. If you have a small crowd, you can allow the ghost two or three chances before having to leave the game. The longest lasting person wins the game.

Murder Mystery Games

If you have ever played a game of Clue, or if you are just fond of trying to solve a challenge, a murder mystery game is perfect for you. It's a game that starts from the moment you arrive at a party and continues until someone has figured out the clues. Creating your own murder mystery isn't as hard as it seems. Knowing how to build the story is key. These games are definitely a great way to keep the guests involved and intrigued throughout the evening.

What You Need

❍ Pen
❍ Paper
❍ Props appropriate for chosen theme

When you send out your invitations to the party, make sure to note that it is a murder mystery party. It's always best to set a theme for a murder mystery. Some popular themes are casino, 1920s, 1950s, Mardi Gras, Halloween, and Western. Having your guests dress the part will help to create a more engaging atmosphere, but it isn't necessary. You will need to create basic character descriptions for each person attending, supplying each character's career and role in the mystery, along with a clue. Here are some examples.

Waiter: You waited on the table of the victim the night of the murder.
Clue: The victim complained about your service, and didn't leave a tip.

Musician: You played piano at the dueling piano bar that the victim frequented every weekend.

Clue: The victim always tipped big, and flaunted money in the bar.

Struggling Comedian: You were the performing act at the location that the victim was murdered.

Clue: The victim was heckling you shortly before the murder.

Lawyer: You were the lawyer for the victim, and his multimillion-dollar company.

Clue: You were aware of all of the victim's offshore accounts, and had access to them.

You will also need filler characters like these: bartender, dancer, elderly couple, private investigator, singer, cousin, etc. Just make sure to create enough to assign each guest a character identity, and these characters should also have a clue that somehow links them to the murderer. That way, when everyone is being questioned, the clues are there to help point out the real murderer.

To begin this murder mystery game, you will need to gather your guests into one room and announce that there has been a murder. You will now say where, when, and how the victim was murdered. Everyone then tries to figure out who the murderer is. Everyone in the room is now a suspect.

Have all the guests close their eyes, and you will circle the room and tap the preplanned murderer on the shoulder. Have them open their eyes and inform them that the person who was tapped is the murderer and it must remain a secret. Supply everyone with a pen and paper for clue gathering.

People will begin their investigations by questioning each other based on the available clues. They are free to implicate anyone in the room they like, to try to throw the scent off them and confuse others. Once everyone has been questioned, and all clues have been gathered, the guests can reveal whom they believe the murderer is. The first person to guess correctly wins the murder mystery game.

Cooking Games

Having people over for dinner is always good fun, but why not switch it up a bit and have everyone join in on the cooking. You can pick a dish of your own, choose a theme for the dinner, or pick out a random recipe. Anything works as long as the guests are having a great time.

Pot Lucky

What You Need

- ○ Disposable dishes and utensils
- ○ Pens
- ○ Paper
- ○ Index cards

This cooking game has you doing little or no cooking, but everyone will get stuffed in the process. Have each guest bring a covered dish (appetizers, sides, meats, and main dishes) and make sure you are the only one to see the dishes. Feel free to make a dish yourself. Number each dish with an index card, and distribute a portion onto plates for each guest.

Place the index card on the table and put the portions in front of it. Give each guest a piece of paper and a pen. Each person will now go station to station trying to guess what is in each dish, and if possible, who made it. The person with the most correct identifications wins the game.

ALERT

Due to food allergies being quite common these days, it would be best to include a note on your invitation regarding the contents of the planned meals. You could also ask guests to acknowledge any allergies when they RSVP.

Ingredients Throw-Down

What You Need

- ○ Timer
- ○ Variety of ingredients
- ○ Cooking utensils

For this lovely little cooking game, you will have your guests helping to prepare dinner and dessert for you. Once all of your guests arrive, you will need to split them up into three groups. One group will be appetizer, one group will be main dish, and the last group will be dessert. Give each group a limited amount of ingredients, and tell them they now have a time limit (thirty minutes for appetizer, one hour for dinner, and one hour for dessert) to create a dish for their category.

They can use any cooking staple they like, such as butter, oil, dressings, and spices. But they have to include each main ingredient you have given them. Once time is up, everyone gets to try the appetizer and judge the dish. Next everyone will enjoy dinner, soon followed by dessert. The most creative and best tasting wins the challenge and can be awarded a prize.

Spice Savvy

What You Need

- ○ Assortment of spicy foods, peppers, and sauces
- ○ Water
- ○ Trashcan

This game is definitely not for the faint of heart—it's for those who enjoy spicy food and don't mind breaking a sweat. Before your guests arrive, prepare a few plates with peppers in one area, spicy sauces in another, and some spicy appetizers in a third area. Your guests will have to challenge one another to a spice match.

For example, someone will pick a person and say, "I bet you couldn't handle a bite of a jalapeño." This person can refuse or accept the challenge. If he accepts, both of them have to take a bite, chew, and swallow without taking a drink or eating a piece of bread for at least a minute after ingestion. If both make it, they move on to another challenge. If either one drinks any liquids before the minute is up, he or she loses. The trashcan is there in case someone needs to spit out the spicy item. The person to ingest the spiciest item or to last the longest wins the game.

ALERT

When experimenting with spicy foods, it is best to make sure that you have a couple of items on hand to ease any discomfort your guests may feel. Milk is good for cooling a spicy tongue, and bread can also help soak up some of the spice. Antacids alleviate any heartburn or indigestion that may arise. Have fun, but safety first!

Cheese Taste-Off

What You Need

○ Pens
○ Paper
○ Glasses of water
○ Plain salt-free crackers
○ Several flavors of cheese

Set up before your guests arrive by laying out the cheese and placing a number in front of each one. You will need to have a master list for yourself with the name of each cheese on it. Have water and crackers laid out so that your guests can clean their palates after each tasting.

When your guests have arrived, give them pen and paper and have them go down the line, sampling each cheese and guessing what cheese it is. This game takes care of an appetizer and entertainment. Once they have all sampled the cheeses and completed the cheese-guessing list, you can see who guessed the most correctly. Then feel free to bring out items that go great with cheese and let the guests enjoy the many flavors.

CHAPTER 11

Getting Married Games

Tying the knot usually consists of a lot of preparation. Even if you are not really that close with the bride or groom, if you have been asked to help with the planning, it can get very overwhelming. In order to alleviate some of the tension and anxiety that tends to occur, try playing some games together.

Engagement Games

Getting engaged is an exciting time for a couple. Announcing the plans to get married is a perfect time to throw a party for the happy pair. But not all engagement parties have to be quiet and reserved. Here are a few games to help with keeping things on the exciting and fun end of the engagement party spectrum.

Who Knows Best

What You Need

- Paper
- Pens
- Small prizes

Start this game off by preparing a list of questions about the bride- and groom-to-be. Include things like where they first met, what their favorite place to eat is, and how long they have had their pet. Once the party is in motion, gather everyone around and give each person a pen and a piece of paper. Read off each question and have the guests write down their answers.

When the guests are done, have people pass their paper to the left of them. You will now reread the question and give the correct answer. They will check the papers, and the person with the most correct answers wins a prize. Tell your guests to feel free to read off any hilarious answers that might have been written down. That's always going to give the happy couple a good chuckle.

Tie the Knot

What You Need

- Garters
- Tape for finish line
- Wedding march music

This is a great game to play outside with your party guests. Use the tape to mark a finish line. Pair up each of your guests and hand each one a garter. They must put the garter around each other's ankles so that they are tied together. When the music starts, the race begins, and the players must rush to the finish line to "tie the knot." The pair to "tie the knot," or cross the finish line first, wins the game.

FACT

The history of the engagement ring goes all the way back to the times of the caveman. They would tie braided cords of grass around their partner's wrist, ankles, and waist in order to gain control of her spirit. And in the first century, puzzle rings were introduced in Asia. The sheiks and sultans used them to mark each of their wives.

Our Future and Then . . .

What You Need

○ Paper
○ Pens
○ Timer

Surely this game will have everyone in stitches once it is done. Have everyone take a pen and paper and have a seat. The object of the game is to start with the phrase "and then." People are to write down two to three sentences describing what the couple will do. They can get as silly as they like with their descriptions. Once everyone is done, you will gather the papers and mix them up. Start telling the story of their future like this: "After the wedding, they drove away together, and then . . ." Now read one of the papers, followed by the next, and continue until you have run out of papers. The story will get everyone giggling about the couple's bright or crazy future together. Who knows, some of it may come true!

Bridal Shower Games

Bridal showers are a time for friends and family of the bride to gather and do something special for the bride that she will always remember. It's the proper way to grace her into the married life. Why not have a few laughs at the same time with these games?

Ring Creation

What You Need

- ❍ Play-Doh or clay
- ❍ Plastic knives
- ❍ Small prize
- ❍ Timer

Everyone will be feeling like a kid again with this game. Give the guests some dough and a plastic knife. They now have three minutes to create a beautiful ring for the bride. They can design the rings however they like to suit her. Once time is up, the bride will judge the rings and pick out the best-looking one. The creator of it wins a small prize.

Gossip

What You Need

- ❍ Index cards
- ❍ Pens

As your guests arrive, have them write down how they know the bride or groom on an index card and return it to you. Once everyone has written down how he or she knows the bride or groom, gather everyone around and give each person an index card (not his or her own). Guests then go around and try to figure out who their card belongs to.

However, they cannot ask anyone "How do you know the bride/groom?" The questions have to be slightly vague. For example, if the card says, "Sara and I were college roommates," the person who got the card must go around and ask questions like, "Did you go to college?" Once everything is winding down, guests can guess who their card belongs to. After the guessing is done, the guests can introduce themselves and how they know the bride or groom.

Bridal Bidding

What You Need

○ Fake money

When you send out your invitations, make sure to ask the guests to bring a small, simple gift that is wrapped. As the guests arrive, take their gift and give them some fake money to bid with. Once all the guests have handed in their gifts and received their money, you can start the bidding. You will hold up a gift and take bids from anyone who wants to buy it. The highest bidder gets the gift. If the player has any leftover money, he or she can give it to someone else for further bidding. When all the guests have their gifts, they can open them.

ESSENTIAL

When sending out your bridal shower invitations, you should make sure that they go out at least a month before the shower. This gives all of the guests ample time to clear their schedules and pick out a gift. It also gives you time to prepare for the shower and to anticipate the party size.

Monkey See, Monkey Do

This game gives the couple the ability to play with their guests. The bride or groom will select a person and whisper something that he or she wants that person to act out to the rest of the group. This person cannot speak, only move around. When someone guesses it correctly, that person now gets to take a turn acting out what the bride or groom tells him or her to do. This continues until everyone has had a turn.

Bachelorette Games

When you hear the words "bachelorette party," your thoughts probably move toward going out on the town and cutting loose. While that is certainly in keeping with the bachelorette tradition, so is game playing. If you are involved in an upcoming bachelorette party, try some of these games out to get things going.

Bachelorette Scavenger Hunt

What You Need

❍ Paper
❍ Pen
❍ Cameras or cell phones

Bachelorette parties usually consist of a night out on the town. Why not do a scavenger hunt while you're at it? Before you all head out for the night, you will need to create a list of things that everyone has to find, and give points for tasks based on how hard they are to complete. It's best to make them silly tasks, such as taking a picture with everyone upside down, getting a group of strangers to spell out YMCA using their arms, snapping a picture of a member in your group that is wearing a strangers hat, or a picture of a fireman pretending to rescue a member of your group.

Ask the guests to get into pairs or groups depending on the size of the party. Give each pair/group a list and a camera, or they can use their cell phones. They now have one hour to try and get as many items on their lists as possible. Select a meeting point and set off to find the items on the list. The team with the most items wins the hunt.

QUESTION

Most Likely

What You Need

○ Pen
○ Paper

Take a minute to write down several different scenarios on pieces of paper, and start each one with "The person who is most likely to . . ." Fold the papers and put them aside. When the guests are ready to play, have them gather around and pick a piece of paper. One by one, each person reads his or her paper, and the guests will shout out the people in the group that they think would be "most likely to." Your guests will be laughing, especially after explaining their guesses and seeing if anyone has done any of the named things.

What's in the Bag?

What You Need

○ Paper
○ Pens
○ Paper bags
○ 5 or more random items (nothing too sharp)

Begin by filling each bag with a random item, and then number the bag. Have the guests line up and give them a piece of paper and a pen. They will each get five seconds to reach into a bag and feel the item without looking. They will then write down the number of the bag and what they believe is inside the bag. The person with the most correct guesses wins.

Bachelor Games

While most of a bachelor party can be consumed by horseplay and shenanigans, getting a few games in that are about marriage should help to keep the boys from getting too out of control.

Being a Bachelor

Have the guys gather around and think of the funniest or most embarrassing moment they have had or had as a bachelor. It can be from teenage years up until the party—as long as it is entertaining, it will do. They will take turns going around and telling their stories to everyone. At the end of the game, the bachelor will decide who had the best story, and that person is the winner.

Musical Identity

This game takes a little preparation on the part of the guests, but it is well worth it in the end. Have each guest pick songs to create a soundtrack for the couple's relationship. Guests are to bring their soundtrack to the party, play it for the bachelor, and give a short description of why they chose those songs. After everyone has played his music, the bachelor will pick the soundtrack that suits the soon-to-be newlyweds best, and that person is the winner. The bachelor can even play it for the bride later, or play it at the reception for all to hear.

QUESTION

What are some different themes used for bachelor parties?
There are some popular themes that can be used to center this special night around. Poker night, camp out, sports, and paintball/laser tag are all great ideas. It's best to base the theme on the personality of the groom.

Advice-and-Sign Challenge

What You Need

○ White T-shirt
○ Permanent marker

If the guys are deciding to hit the town, this will give them a challenge to complete while out having fun. The bachelor must wear the white T-shirt and take the marker with him. While they are out and about, the bachelor has to get at least fifty people to give him marriage advice and write it on his shirt. Things such as "Know when to choose your battles," "Never go to sleep angry," and "Whatever you do, don't forget your anniversary!"

It's best to set rewards for certain amounts of signage for the bachelor; that way, he is on a mission. You can set the standard for the signing totals and prizes as you please. Some good prize ideas you could use are gift cards, movies, and T-shirts.

Rehearsal Dinner Games

Rehearsal dinners sometimes function as the event that allows for both sides of family and friends to meet for the first time. That also means trying to make it through dinner with minimal amounts of tension and awkwardness. A couple of games to get the crowd introduced and involved will help.

Something in Common

When you prepare your seating arrangements for the rehearsal, seat your guests by something that they all have in common. You can have a table of people in the same profession, people who love to ski, people with the same zodiac sign, etc. The guests' job is to converse with one another and try to find out what it is that they all have in common. This will make for a more relaxed dinner. The table to guess their interest first wins the game.

FACT

Weddings in India are very rich with tradition and meaning. They have a *jaimala*, which is an exchange of beautiful flower garlands. They also do *Gathbandhan*—when married, the bride and groom's hands are bound with a scarf to express their eternal bond, their promise to be faithful, and their love for one another forever.

Shoes Up

This is an adorable game that involves the bride and the groom and how they see their relationship. Place two chairs back-to-back and have the bride sit in one chair and the groom sit in the other. Have them take their shoes off and hand one shoe to the other person. They will need to hold one of their shoes in one hand and their partner's shoe in the other hand. You will then ask them a series of questions, and they will hold up the shoe of the person who the question pertains to.

For example, you could ask, "Who does the dishes most between the two of you?" They will then hold up the shoe of who they believe does the dishes the most. Have someone keep score on how many times they agree during the questioning. Everyone will be laughing by the end of the questions. You can even have the guests ask a couple of questions of their own.

Thank-You Raffle

What You Need

- ❍ Envelopes
- ❍ Pens
- ❍ Basket
- ❍ A prize or prizes

This raffle will take care of getting addresses of everyone for thank-you notes. Have all the guests put their addresses on an envelope and drop them in the basket. At the end of the rehearsal dinner, you will draw a name or a couple of names and hand out the gift(s).

Getting-to-Know-the-In-Laws Games

In-laws are going to be a part of a married couple's life from the moment the couple says "I do." So what better way to get familiar than through game play? After all, who doesn't want to see what they are getting themselves into when extending the family?

Picture Pairs

What You Need

- ○ Assorted pictures of the couple
- ○ Scissors
- ○ Envelopes

You will need to gather pictures that can be cut for this game. If you have thirty guests attending, you will need fifteen pictures. Cut each picture in half and put each half in its own envelope. As your guests arrive to the gathering, hand them an envelope. Make sure they know that only they get to see what is inside. They must go around and mingle with others, asking simple questions about their photos to see if they can find their other half.

Giving a time limit sometimes makes it easier on everyone, but it is up to you. Announce when the game is through and see who can correctly guess who has their other half. This will get everyone talking and getting to know one another.

FACT

In Russia, grooms must work to get their brides. They show up at the family's home and ask for the bride, and cannot have her until they have endured being humiliated and/or given the bride's family plenty of gifts. Once the family feels satisfied, they release the bride to the groom for them to join one another in marriage.

The Name Game

Ask guests to stand up one by one and say their name. The catch is that they must add an adjective that describes their character, and it has to start with the same letter as their first name. So if there is an Amy, she can say, "Hi, I am amusing Amy." When the guests are done, they will need to refer to each other by their new names for the rest of the night. This helps to reveal a little about your guests' personalities.

String Thing

What You Need

○ String
○ Scissors

This game will have all of the guests wondering what you're up to. Pass the spool of string around, and have people cut pieces of any size they like. Do not hint or reveal why they are cutting these pieces of string, or it will ruin the game. Once everyone has his or her string, announce what the purpose of the game is. One by one, the guests will stand up and start to wrap the string around their finger. While doing this, the people will have to talk about themselves until they are finishing wrapping the string. This helps everyone get familiar with each other, without having to ask too many questions.

Wedding Reception Games

Now that the most important and precious part of the whole wedding is over, it's time to celebrate! With every guest in high spirits and ready to get down a little, it's time to really get things going!

Advice Tables

What You Need

- ❍ Mini notebooks
- ❍ Pens

This takes a little bit of preparation, but is a sweet gift for the bride and groom. For each table at the reception, you will leave a mini notebook with a question on the front of it and several pens. The questions should be based on things people often need input on. Questions like, "What should we do to celebrate our one-year anniversary?" "What are some fun things to do on free nights?" "Where should we go for our first vacation?" and "What are some ways to avoid long-lasting arguments?" The guests will write their advice in the notebooks for the bride and groom to read at a later date.

Face Off

What You Need

- ❍ Towel rods or paint stirrers
- ❍ Photos of the bride's face and the groom's face
- ❍ Printer
- ❍ Glue or tape
- ❍ Scissors

This game will have the bride and groom laughing it up when they realize how others view them in certain situations. To prepare, you will need to print enough pictures of the bride's and groom's faces so that every guest will get one of each. Once they are printed, you will need to trim out just the face of each person and glue or tape it to the stick. When laying out the reception dining ware, you will put one picture of the bride's face and one of the groom's at each plate.

When the game starts, the bride and groom will meet in the middle of the room and be seated next to one another. You will explain to the guests that you are going to ask some questions about the bride and groom. Whoever they believe is more likely to be the one in question is the face they are to hold up.

While in America it is tradition to toss a bouquet after the wedding, it is different in some countries. In Peru, they do a cake-pull, where ribbons are baked into the cake and a piece of each ribbon is hanging out of the cake. The women will pick a string and pull, and the one to retrieve a fake wedding ring attached to her string is said to be the next to marry.

For example, if you asked, "Who is more likely to steal a parking space?" The guests will hold up the face for the person they think would be most likely to do it. The bride and groom may be surprised by some of the answers of their family and friends.

Sit Down, Stand Up

Inform your guests that they are to stand up at their tables. Either give a list of questions to someone who will read them off, or you read the list to everyone. All the questions will require the guests to stand or sit. The first question could start like this: "If you have known the bride for more than five years, sit down." Then follow up with another question pertaining to the couple and ask those people to stand up. This will get people familiar with one another to learn a little about each other and the roles that they play in the couple's life.

CHAPTER 12

Baby Shower Games

The arrival of a baby is a blessing, and one of the few things celebrated long before and long after the birth. Baby showers are a way to celebrate the love surrounding such an amazing time. Games are definitely the focal point of most baby showers. They keep mommy laughing, memories flowing, and anticipation at an all-time high. Help everyone to enjoy the coming of the precious bundle by playing a few of these games.

Gender-Reveal Games

A gender-reveal party is a great way to get everyone together and disclose the gender of the new baby/babies all at once. That way there is no need to worry about whom to call and tell first. Another great thing about this type of party is that it can be just for the people closest to the parent/parents.

Old Wives' Tales

What You Need

○ Small prizes

This game will need to be played before the gender of the baby has been revealed. Also, the rewards for these games will be given out only after the gender has been revealed to everyone. Have everyone who is playing the game gather around. You are going to use old wives' tales that try to predict the sex of the baby. Take suggestions from the players about things they believe hint at what gender the baby might be.

Some classic old wives' tales are that what the mother craves tells you the gender—sweets usually indicate a girl, and spicy foods, a boy. Carrying a baby high up in the stomach is supposed to be telling of a girl, and carrying the baby lower means a boy. Tie a ring to a string and hold it over the mother's belly; if it swings back and forth, it's a girl, and if it swings in a circle, it's a boy. Once all the old wives' tales have been told, everyone guesses the baby's gender; after the reveal, those who were right will get a prize.

ESSENTIAL

Did you know that you can take your ultrasound to a bakery and they will bake you a cake that is tinted inside based on the sex of the baby? That way, you find out the gender along with everyone else. Another fun way to find out is to have pink or blue helium balloons filled and placed in a box to be opened when everyone has arrived.

Pop and Reveal

What You Need

- ○ Latex balloons (dark, non-gender-specific color)
- ○ Blue or pink confetti (based on the gender of the baby)

This game is for someone who already knows the sex of the baby. You will need to fill the balloons with air, and just one of the balloons will have confetti placed inside of it before blowing it up. Spread the balloons around all over the floor; using a lot of balloons makes it even more entertaining.

When you are ready to reveal the gender, have all the guests begin stomping on the balloons to find the one with the confetti in it. The person who pops the right balloon gets the prize of announcing the gender to the rest of the crowd.

Tally Up

What You Need

- ○ Chalkboard or poster board
- ○ Chalk or marker

Hang the chalkboard or poster board right inside the entrance doorway. Draw a line down the middle and write "girl" on one side and "boy" on the other. As the guests arrive, they are to put a tally mark on the side that they believe is the gender of the baby. Before the reveal happens, count up the tallies, then announce the final total for both genders. Announce the sex of the baby, and see if the majority of the guests were right or wrong.

Boy Games

If a little bundle of boy is expected, there are ways to create the right atmosphere for your little man's welcoming. While decorations and food can be handled easily by color and taste, games can be geared to focus on your baby boy and get you ready for what playtime might be like with him.

Boy-Word Jumble

What You Need

○ Computer with printer
○ Paper
○ Pens
○ Timer

For this game, you will need to produce a list of words that typically pertain to boys (cars, sports, dirt, blue, etc.). Number the page from one to ten. Then make another list that jumbles up each word's lettering, so you can't make out the words. Print out a copy of the jumbled-words list for each guest attending.

Give each guest a list of jumbled words, face down, and a pen. Set the timer for one minute. When you start the timer, your guests will turn over their papers and begin to decipher the words. The one to finish the fastest, with the most correct solutions, wins the game.

QUESTION

Other than the traditional blue, what are some acceptable colors for a baby boy shower?
Gender usually plays heavy into a baby shower. With boys you can use shades of green, brown, ivory, and yellow if you are trying to stay away from traditional blue. You can also incorporate several of the colors to give a little more color to the baby scheme.

Tales of Boys

Having a little boy is very different from having a little girl. Have your guests gather around and tell the most entertaining story about their sons, brothers, or other male siblings from when they were young. This will help prepare mommy for what to expect with having a boy. The mother will then judge who had the funniest story, and he or she will win a small prize.

Baby Boy Name Game

What You Need

- ○ Paper
- ○ Pens
- ○ Timer
- ○ Small gift

Have the guests gather around and give them a pen and paper. Assign each a letter in the alphabet. Make sure not to give anyone the same letter. Set the timer for two minutes, and when it starts, the guests must try to think of as many boy names that start with the letter of the alphabet they were given. The person with the most names on his or her list wins a prize.

Girl Games

Since mommies already know what it's like to be a girl, planning a shower for a girl won't be too hard. But finding the right girly games for guests may be a bit hard. Here a few game suggestions to make things easier.

Is It a Girl?

What You Need

- ○ Pictures of babies in which gender is hard to identify
- ○ Large poster board
- ○ Marker
- ○ Pens
- ○ Paper

When preparing this game, you will need to locate pictures of babies that are hard to tell if it's a boy or a girl. Hang the pictures up on the poster board and place a number over the top of the picture. When you are ready to begin playing, you will need to give each guest a pen and a piece of paper.

They must guess if the babies in the pictures are boys or girls. The one with most correct gender guesses wins the game.

What Was Mommy Wearing?

What You Need

○ Pens
○ Paper

Have everyone converse with each other, including mommy, for about twenty minutes. Then secretly ask mommy to leave the room. Gather the guests around, and give everyone a pen and paper. Ask them the following questions (if they apply, or make up your own), and tell them to write down their answers on the paper.

- What was mommy wearing?
- What color/colors was she wearing?
- What jewelry did she have on?
- What color was her nail polish?
- What shoes did she have on?
- How was her hair styled?
- What color was her lipstick?
- What color was her eye shadow?

Once you have asked all of the questions, have mommy come back into the room, reveal the answers, and have the guests check their sheets. The player(s) with the most correct answers win(s) the game.

ALERT

When planning a baby shower, you will need to be considerate of the mother-to-be when deciding the menu. Try to keep anything spicy, heavy, or caffeinated off the menu so that she can enjoy her meal without having to be worried about what she ate that upset her stomach and baby.

Songs for a Girl

What You Need

○ Pens
○ Paper
○ Timer

When the guests are ready to play the game, have them take a seat and hand each one a pen and paper. Set the timer for two minutes and tell the players that when the timer starts, they have to write down as many songs as they can that contain a girl's name in the title of the song. The person with the most songs listed wins.

Silly Baby Shower Games

Just the idea of a sweet little baby being brought into the world can give you a giddy feeling inside. Why not continue that feeling with a few games? Getting mama to giggle a bit is always a bonus at a shower.

Feed Me!

What You Need

○ Assortment of jarred baby food
○ Spoons
○ Blindfolds
○ Bibs

This is a hysterical game for the guests to get a little messy. Start by having your guests break into pairs. One of the pair will put on a blindfold and the other will put on a bib. The blindfolded person will be handed a spoon and a jar of baby food. They will be racing against the others to feed their partner as fast as they can without making a huge mess. You can do a second round by letting them switch positions and go again. The one with the quickest feed time and the least mess win the game.

ESSENTIAL

Another version of this game is to remove the labels on the jars and have the guests take turns trying the flavors. They will write down their guesses, and the one that has the most correct guesses at the end of the testing wins the game.

Bottle Guzzle

What You Need

○ Several cheap baby bottles with nipples
○ Milk or drink of your choice

Begin by preparing each bottle and filling it with the drink you have chosen. Have the players stand in a line side by side, and hand each one a bottle. When the game begins they will have to guzzle the drink from the bottle, like a baby, as fast as they can. The person to finish the bottle first wins the game.

Change Me, Mommy!

What You Need

○ Toilet paper
○ Timer

Separate your guests into pairs and give them each a roll of toilet paper. One of them will be mommy and the other the baby. Set the timer for two minutes and tell the pairs they have two minutes to wrap the baby in a diaper made from the toilet paper. When the time is up, mommy gets to judge each diaper and pick a winner for best-looking diaper.

Baby Shower Guessing Games

The following games are perfect if you are planning a baby shower with the intention of giving out prizes. If you'd like, you can combine the prizes and the guessing game itself to save time and money. This will make things a little bit easier on you in the long run.

Baby Face

What You Need

- ❍ Pictures of guests as babies
- ❍ Poster board
- ❍ Tape
- ❍ Pens
- ❍ Paper

When you send out the invitations, ask the guests to supply you with a picture of them as a child. Tape each picture to the poster board and put a number above it. When the guests arrive, have them take a pen and paper and write down which guests they believe the pictures are of. The player with the most correct guesses wins.

The Book Exchange

When you send out the invitations for the shower, ask guests to bring a children's book that suits their personality best. When the guests arrive, have them place the books in a pile, and do not reveal which person brought which book. When the guest of honor is done opening her gifts, she can begin going through the books. She must try to guess the person she thinks brought each book, and give an explanation as to why she thinks it is that person. She then gets to keep the books to read to baby!

Dirty Diapers

What You Need

- ❍ Baby diapers (one for each type of candy)
- ❍ Variety of chocolate candy bars (at least four different candy bars)
- ❍ Permanent marker
- ❍ Enough pens and pencils for each guest
- ❍ One piece of paper for each guest

This is one of the funniest baby shower games you can play. It always grosses out a few, but it's in good fun. You will need to number the diapers on the outside, using the marker. Put a piece of the chocolate bar into the first diaper, and heat it up in the microwave for five-second increments, until melted. Do this for each numbered diaper, using a different candy for each one, making sure to keep track of what number is what candy.

To start the game, have everyone sit at a table, and beginning with diaper number one, start passing it around. The players will sniff the dirty diaper and write down what candy they believe is inside the diaper. The player with the most correct guesses wins.

Mommy's Tummy

What You Need

- ❍ Toilet paper

Have the guest of honor stand in front of everyone, and give the roll of toilet paper to one of the guests. That person must pull off as many sheets as he or she thinks it would take to go around mommy's tummy. Once everyone has his or her sheets pulled, use the toilet paper to measure her stomach. Compare that amount to everyone else's, and the person with the closest amount wins the game.

Baby Shower Action Games

While it is always nice to sit around, eat some cake, and trade a few birthing stories, being active is also great entertainment. Use the following games to get your shower guests up and out of their seats, vying for a few prizes.

Bottle Bowling

What You Need

- ❍ 10 baby bottles
- ❍ Baseball or tennis ball

To set this game up, you will need to fill each bottle about a quarter of the way full with water and put the top on. Line up the bottles like you would bowling pins. Give the first player the ball. That person has two tries to knock down as many bottles as he or she can. Once everyone has had a turn, the player with the highest score wins the game.

ESSENTIAL

You can cut costs with a baby shower by shopping at your local dollar store or discount store for supplies. You can find everything from favors, food supplies, gift-wrap, and décor. That way, your wallet isn't empty, and you have one less thing to stress over!

Baby Change Challenge

What You Need

- ❍ Baby doll, dressed

- ○ Diapers
- ○ Blanket
- ○ Timer

This is a good challenge for the seasoned pros. Each participant will take turns undressing the baby, changing its diaper, redressing, and swaddling the baby while being timed. There is one rule, however, which is that the baby must be treated as if it were real. Players must not be careless just to finish quickly. The player with the fastest time wins the game.

Spit the Pacifier

What You Need

- ○ Several pacifiers

This competitive game will have the guests working on their spitting skills. Have everyone line up at an established starting line. When the game starts, the players will put a pacifier in their mouth and spit it as far as they can. The player who spits his or her pacifier the farthest wins the game.

Baby Shower Thinking Games

Testing the minds of your guests at a baby shower can lead to a thousand laughs. You can touch on anything from their knowledge of current trends to how well they know the mother-to-be. Tell your guests to dig deep on these games and prove just how much they know!

On the Line

What You Need

- ○ String
- ○ Clothespins
- ○ Pens
- ○ Paper

○ Assortment of baby items

Before the guests arrive, put the string up across the room like you would a clothesline. Pin the baby items along the string. Allow everyone to come in and mingle for about twenty minutes before you take the clothesline down and put it out of everyone's sight. Now give the players a piece of paper and a pen, and have them write down all the items that they remember being on the line. The player with the most correct items wins. The mommy gets to take home all the baby items that were on the line.

Nursery Rhyme Time

What You Need

○ Computer and printer
○ Paper
○ Pens

On your computer, you will need to compile a list of lines from nursery rhymes. You should do at least ten different rhymes on your list. Print out a copy for each guest attending the shower. Give the guests a list and a pen; they must now try to figure out what nursery rhymes the lines belong to. The player with the most correct guesses wins the game.

FACT

Did you know that the most popular day that babies are born is on a Tuesday? Monday is the next favored day. Sunday falls in as the least popular for babies to make their entrance into the world. The most popular month is September, followed by August, June, and then July.

Babies, Babies, Babies

What You Need

○ Computer with printer

○ Paper
○ Pens

Create a list of animals and leave a space next to each animal name to write down the correct name of its baby. Some examples are kangaroo (joey), dog (puppy), cat (kitten), bear (cub), bat (pup), cow (calf), and ape (baby). Using more exotic animals will have the guests racking their brains. Print out a sheet for each guest, and when you start the game, give the guests a paper and a pen. They must guess as many animals as they can. The one with the most identified wins the game.

Baby Shower Sentimental Games

Having a baby is indeed a sentimental time for all mothers. These games and activities are focused on reminding the guest of honor how wonderful her journey is going to be.

Time Capsule

What You Need

○ A lock box or something to act as the capsule
○ Items for the capsule

When you send out your invitations, ask the guests to bring something sentimental to put in your capsule. It can be anything that would be interesting to the child once he or she is old enough to open it. Gather all of the things together and have Mommy decide a time for her child to open the capsule and go through all the things people wanted her to see. Pictures of Mommy with friends, jewelry, news articles, money with the year of the child's birth on it, and music are all great items to use.

ALERT

When playing a game with an item that can also be a gift to the mother, like the time capsule game, make sure you set the gift aside. Things can get a bit hectic during the cleanup of a baby shower, especially if you are on a time limit. You want to make sure the gift is not taken out with the trash or given away to one of the other guests.

Mommy-to-Be Memory

This can get the tears going a bit if played. All of the guests will take turns talking about how they met Mommy and a special memory they have of her. Once they have gone around the room, Mommy must then go around and tell everyone a special memory that she has about each person.

Wish Jar

What You Need

○ Scraps of paper
○ Pens
○ Mason jar

You can choose to decorate the jar or to leave it plain, but you might want to at least write "wish jar" on it. Leave the wish jar by the entrance and as the guests enter, they are to write down a wish that they have for the baby on a scrap of paper and place it in the jar. They can be wishes such as traveling, falling in love, and never giving up on anything he or she is passionate about. After everyone is done, give the jar to the mother-to-be; she can open it and read it to the child when the child is a bit older and able to understand the wishes everyone had for him or her.

CHAPTER 13

Decade Party Games

There is nothing quite as entertaining as a decade party. It's always fun to relive the past, especially if it's a time period with funny clothing and music. Costumes and decorations make the theme, but what about entertainment? Try some games, of course!

Venetian Masquerade Games

If you are planning a masquerade party, you are in for a night of intrigue. Most of the time the mission of the attendees is to dress so that no one knows who they are. The following games use this concept to create a fun and mysterious evening.

ESSENTIAL

Sometimes it can be hard to find decorations or costume supplies for a Venetian theme. You can almost always use items that are for or from Mardi Gras for these games. There is a great selection of masks available in the Mardi Gras section of costume stores and online.

Who's Behind the Mask?

What You Need

○ Paper
○ Pens

Ask your guests to dress in costume and wear their masks. As the guests arrive, give them a pen and paper and ask them not to speak for the first couple of minutes of the party. The players are to go around and try to identify who each guest is without speaking. They will write their guesses down and hand their papers to the host. The player with the most correct guesses wins.

Mask Creations

What You Need

○ Plain paper mache mask
○ Low-temp glue gun
○ Sequins, jewels, feathers, and glitter

This can be done while the party is going on. Have all the supplies out on a table and the glue gun plugged in. Invite the guests to stop by the station and add to the mask what they want. Once everyone has added to the mask, it will be presented to the host as a thank-you for the invitation to the party.

Roaring '20s Games

Flappers, gangsters, and movies stars were all so popular during this era. The 1920s were a booming time for automobiles and radio as well. A party theme of this caliber has endless possibilities and potential. Try out a few of these original games to get the party started right.

Boa Limbo

What You Need

❍ Feathered boa
❍ 1920s music

This is a very entertaining twist on a classic game. Take two volunteers to hold the boa during the game. Have all the players line up and start the music. The players are to limbo underneath the boa without touching it and then return to the back of the line. This continues until there is only one person left who is able to limbo. This person is the winner of the boa limbo.

FACT

The 1920s were a time for huge transition in the United States. For the very first time, more people were moving into the city instead of living out on farms. This was the time of the flapper, a female who wore short hair and glittery dresses. While most people found this time to be a troubling one, the young definitely saw it as hoppin' and roarin'.

1920s Dance-Off

What You Need

- ○ 1920s music
- ○ Prizes

When you are sending out your invitations, mention that there will be a 1920s dance-off. Give guests a choice of the following dances to learn and compete with: the Fox Trot, the Charleston, the Turkey Trot, and the Black Bottom. When the party starts, invite the guests to compete in the dance-off. Those who are not participating will be the judges. The winners get to take home a prize.

Groovy '60s Games

A '60s party! Whoa man, that's heavy stuff. With a party like this, anticipate pinups, poodle skirts, and the hippie period. Those were times of rock-and-roll and self-discovery. Take everyone back in your party time-machine with a couple of these groovy games.

What's That Line?

What You Need

- ○ 1960s music and player
- ○ Prize

If your guests are familiar with popular music from the '60s, they will love this challenge. Cue up a song and have a player stand up to sing. Play the song, and the person must sing along. Pause the song whenever you like, and the player must finish the next line of the song in order to move on to the next round. Continue with rounds until it is down to two people competing. They will challenge one another until someone doesn't know the line. The winner takes home a prize.

Is the hippie style the only fashion that you can use to celebrate the 1960s?
No! The '60s was a time when fashion transitioned from poodle skirts, ponytails, and saddle shoes into the more extreme fashion that we associate with it. While hippie bell-bottoms, peace signs, long hair, and afros were all the rage, there were also other fashion trends coming into the spotlight. "Mod" was another popular fashion that included miniskirts with go-go boots!

Stay in Character

As your guests arrive, let them know that there is a game they can play or just help with if they like. The game is that the players have to stay in character and talk (using hippie accents and lingo) like they are from the '60s for as long as they can. If anyone drops character and is caught, he or she is out of the game. The person to last the longest wins the game.

Disco '70s Games

Disco was quite the rage in the 1970s. It was a time of platform shoes, afros, and disco balls. A disco party is something no one will want to miss. So break out your disco ball, start stretching, and don't forget your thermometer, because everyone is going to catch the boogie fever!

Poptastic Afro

What You Need

○ Afro wigs
○ Popped popcorn
○ Timer

You will need to split your guests into teams for this game. Give each team an afro wig and a bag of popcorn. Set your timer at two minutes, and have the teams pick one person to wear the afro. Have the person wearing the wig sit on the floor about five to six feet from the rest of his or her group. When the timer starts, the team members will take turns throwing one piece of popcorn at a time at the afro. When the time is up, the afro with the most popcorn in it is the winning team.

ALERT

While in adulthood it is rather uncommon for people to carry lice, it isn't so uncommon in childhood. You're always better safe than sorry. Wig caps can be worn if wigs are going to be shared. Also, knowing your crowd and having extra wigs, while staying within your financial means, will help to lessen the risk of sharing the wigs with one another.

Dress-and-Dash Relay

What You Need

○ Leisure suit
○ Afro
○ Platform shoes
○ Timer

This game will have you either raiding the closet for old gear or visiting a vintage clothing store. Either way this game is a blast. Put the clothing items on one side of the room and have the guests stand on the other. Have the players split into teams.

The first team will step up, and when the timer starts, one player will run across the room and put all the items on as fast as he or she can. That person will then run to the team and back to where you've placed the clothes and quickly get undressed.

Once that person returns to the team, the next player does the same thing. This continues until every player has had a turn or until the timer stops. The next team will take their turn and try to beat that team's time. The team with the best time wins the challenge.

Totally '80s Games

Ever wonder what your friends would look like dressed up like an '80s hair band? The '80s consisted of fishnets, long hair, tons of hairspray, and ripped clothing, making it a time few could forget. These games are centered on the best of the '80s; try them out on your guests and see if you can get a few flashbacks going!

Pin the Mullet on the Dude

What You Need

- ❍ Large picture of a bald guy dressed like he's from the '80s
- ❍ Cutout of a mullet
- ❍ Double-sided tape
- ❍ Blindfold

This is a spin on a classic game most everyone is familiar with: Pin the Tail on the Donkey. Since mullets were all the rage in the '80s, this is the perfect game for your party. Have your guests line up to take a shot at pinning the mullet on the dude. Each player will take turns putting on the blindfold and trying to pin the mullet on the best they can. The player with the closest pin wins the game.

ESSENTIAL

Having an '80s party is always better with some background music. Most stores carry mixed CDs for different eras. Just having the music play in the background helps to set the mode for the party theme itself.

Rubik's Cube Challenge

What You Need

- ❍ Rubik's Cube

○ Timer

The Rubik's cube was a huge hit in the '80s. Give your guests a chance to try to solve the cube while the timer is going. The person with the best time gets to take the cube home as a prize.

Hip-Hop and Punk '90s Games

If any generation strived to create its own style, the '90s did it, several times over. Anything from backward clothing, sagging pants, flannels, and ripped jeans, the '90s generation tried it all. From the economy to the fashion world, everything was booming in the '90s and opened doors to endless possibilities, so your party should as well. Bring your guests back to this exciting era by playing a few of these fun-filled '90s-era games.

Who Am I?

What You Need

○ Safety pins
○ Paper
○ Marker
○ Prizes

Write down the name of a popular celebrity of the '90s on each of the sheets of paper. As your guests arrive, pin a name on their back so they cannot see who they are. They can ask questions about themselves, but no one can reveal who they are—they must figure it out on their own. The first couple of guests who figure out their identity win a prize.

FACT

Rap really hit hard in the '90s, taking music by storm. Did you know that in 1990, Vanilla Ice was the first rap artist to have a number one rap single? That's right; "Ice Ice Baby" was playing on everyone's radio then.

'90s Musical Charades

What You Need

- ○ Paper
- ○ Pen
- ○ Bowl

Write down the names of several bands from the '90s—ranging from boy bands, rap groups, and punk music—on separate pieces of paper, fold, and place in the bowl. Have your guests gather around and split into groups. Have the members of the group take turns pulling a paper from the bowl.

The players must then act out the artist they pulled to get their team to guess who they are before the other team guesses. The catch in this game is that the players can hum the songs of the artists they pull, and they can also imitate their dance moves for the audience, but they cannot speak. The team with the most correct guesses wins the game.

CHAPTER 14

Holiday Games

Holidays usually bring about a feeling of joy, but they can sometimes cause unnecessary stress. They don't always have to revolve around spending a ton of money and feeling overwhelmed. Even if it is a simple night with the family, playing a game during the holiday season will put anyone in a great mood. Try a couple of great games to get the holiday spirit up and going.

Valentine's Day Games

This day is not just for lovers, it's a day for all of us to take time to show that we care about one another. Whether it's for the classroom, at home, or the office, playing a few games will get everyone smiling.

Catch My Heart

What You Need

○ Stuffed "Valentine" animals

Get all of the players to spread out around a room. Hand one of the stuffed animals to a player. The player must call out the name of someone in the group and toss him or her the animal. That person must then do the same thing. If anyone drops the animal, that person is out of the game. Once everyone is familiar with the game and how it is played, you will throw in another stuffed animal. Play continues and speeds up a bit until all are out but the last two—they are the winners of the game.

Broken Hearted

What You Need

○ Paper hearts
○ Scissors
○ Bowl

Cut the paper hearts in half, making sure to use different cutting designs for each one. Stick the broken hearts in a bowl and mix them up. Have the players gather around the bowl and pick a half heart out of the bowl. They now have to try and hunt down the other half of their heart. The first to find the other half of his or her broken heart wins the game.

FACT

Cupid, who is usually associated with Valentine's Day, dates back to Roman mythology. He was the son of Venus, the goddess of love. The Greeks knew Cupid as Eros, the son of Aphrodite. He would shoot arrows to pierce people's hearts so they would fall in love.

Sweets Race

What You Need

- ○ Small disposable cups
- ○ Candy
- ○ Timer
- ○ Bowl for each team

Have your guests split up into teams. Place a bowl across the room from each team and give the team a cup and some candy. One at a time, players from each team must fill up the cup with candy using their hands, place it on their head, walk across the room without touching the cup on their head, and dump it into their team's bowl on the other side. If they drop the cup, they must go back and fill up and start again. This play continues for three minutes. At the end of that time, the game is over and the team with the most candy wins.

Where Is Cupid?

What You Need

- ○ Scraps of paper
- ○ Pen
- ○ Bowl

This is a good game to use as an icebreaker if the players are not that familiar with one another. Draw hearts on the pieces of scrap paper. On one of the cards, in the center of one of the hearts, write the letter C. Fold up the papers and place them in a bowl.

When the guests are ready to play the game, explain that they are going to pull a piece of paper, and if they have the letter C on theirs, then they are Cupid. They must keep what is on their paper to themselves.

Now the guests will go around shaking each other's hands, and the person who is Cupid will slyly choose one person to tickle the palm or wrist of the person he or she is shaking hands with. This person whose hand was tickled will, quietly, go have a seat while others continue to play. Guests must try to guess who Cupid is before they shake hands and are out of the game. When someone discovers Cupid, the game starts all over again.

Easter Games and Hunts

Spring, pastel colors, bunnies, and colored eggs are all parts of Easter. While traditional egg hunts are a blast to experience, mixing things up a bit and trying something new can get everyone hyped for this upcoming Easter. Here are a few must-try hunts, games, and activities to get Easter started right.

Egg Roller Relay

What You Need

○ Hard-boiled Easter eggs, one for each player

Give each player an egg, and have everyone go to the starting line. The object of the game is to roll your egg from the starting line to the finish line and back without cracking the shell. Base the distance between the start and finish line on the age of the participants.

Of course, if they are very young, a short distance will work. The older they are, the farther apart you can set the lines. You can choose to have the players roll the egg using only their noses, one finger, or feet—whatever you want. The person who finishes first is, of course, the winner of the relay!

Egg Pass

What You Need

○ Boiled eggs or plastic eggs

Have the participants separate into at least two groups. Have the groups line up so they are side by side with their team members. Give each team an egg. The object of this game is to have to players put the egg in between their chin and neck and pass it to the person next to them. They must retrieve the egg using their chin and neck and continue to pass it on the same way. If someone drops the egg, that person must start over. The first team to pass the egg all the way down without dropping it wins the game.

ESSENTIAL

Easter is a time of decorating boiled eggs. Most of these eggs just get set aside and wasted. The great thing about Easter games is that you can use the decorated eggs in place of plastic eggs. They also are great substitutes for eggs in an Easter egg hunt.

Carrot Toss

What You Need

○ Carrots
○ Hula-Hoops

Begin by laying the Hula-Hoops four or five feet apart from one another. Split the kids into teams and give them a bunch of carrots to share. The game starts with one person from each team standing about six feet from the Hula-Hoop. Each player must toss his or her carrot and try to land it inside of the hoop.

When a player misses, the next person will go but must take a step back before tossing. If that person makes the toss, he or she receives a point for the team and the next person goes. After everyone has tossed once or twice, the team with the most points wins the game.

A Different Kind of Hunt

Doing the same kind of egg hunt every Easter is always fun, but if you want to switch things up a bit this year, there are a couple different ways you can do this. One idea is to do a hunt when it is about to get dark out. You can hand out flashlights or you can use glow-in-the-dark eggs for the kids to find. Another idea is to have the eggs be color coordinated. In this game, every child is assigned an egg color and has to find all his or her eggs before anyone else. The first to find all of his or her colored eggs wins the hunt.

Puzzle and Clue Hunt

What You Need

○ Easter puzzle
○ Marker
○ Plastic eggs

Purchase an Easter puzzle, put it together, and write a location on the back in marker. Take the puzzle apart and put a puzzle piece in each plastic egg and hide them around the yard with empty eggs. You can tell the children that they have to piece together a puzzle in order to find the hidden candy treasure. Once all the pieces have been found, have them work with one another to put the puzzle together, and flip it over to read the location of the candy treasure. And if you want to incorporate the story of Easter, you can stuff the eggs with lines from the story. After all the eggs are found, the kids can put the story in the right order and read it aloud to everyone. If you are working with a younger crowd, you may want to number the eggs so that putting the story together is a bit easier on them.

Halloween Games

Halloween is a great excuse to carve a pumpkin, dress up, and get free candy. Where can you sign up, right? While being scared can be quite the adrenaline rush, it isn't always a necessity when celebrating this holiday. It doesn't matter if you are young or old—break out your costume, get a good sugar rush going, and play some Halloween games to get this holiday on track!

Mummy Wrap

What You Need

❍ Toilet paper

For this entertaining little game you will need players to split into teams. Give each team a roll of toilet paper. They must wrap up one of their teammates like a mummy, using the entire roll of toilet paper. The first team to wrap their mummy from head to toe is the winner of the game.

Eyeball Dig

What You Need

❍ Ping-Pong balls
❍ Spaghetti noodles
❍ Large bowl
❍ Colored markers

This game requires a little bit of preparation beforehand, but it is a riot to watch. Start by boiling the noodles, and once done, drain them and place them in a bowl. Using the colored markers, draw a small circle on each ball, using different colors. Develop a point system, making each color a different amount of points. Mix the "eyeballs" in with the noodles in the bowl.

When the guests are ready to play, you will set your timer at forty-five seconds. Have the first player put on the blindfold and when the time starts, the person will dig through the noodles trying to get as many eyeballs as he or she can. When that person is done, tally up the points, and let the next player take a turn getting eyeballs. The player with the most points at the end of the game wins.

Mr. Bones Skeleton Hunt

What You Need

- ○ Large plastic skeleton or skeleton cutout
- ○ Pen
- ○ Paper
- ○ Candy

If you are using a plastic skeleton, you will need to separate the bones. If you are using a paper skeleton, you will need to cut out and separate the bones. You are going to hide the bones all over the game area. Before you begin your hunt, let the players know that they are on a bone hunt. Mr. Bones has fallen apart and needs to be put back together in order to share his treasures of candy.

ESSENTIAL

If you do not want to use a skeleton for your hunt, you can use Frankenstein's monster. Just separate his body and hide the pieces all over the play area. You can even have the participants pretend they are mad Dr. Frankensteins "creating" their own monster.

Ghosts and Goblins

What You Need

- ○ A small picture of a ghost (about the size of an index card), photocopied or drawn enough times for half of your players to have four copies each
- ○ A small picture of a goblin (or other spooky creature, about the size of an index card), photocopied or drawn enough times for half of your players to have four copies each
- ○ Scissors
- ○ Ball of string or yarn
- ○ Hole punch

After a good sugar rush from eating Halloween candy, players can burn off some of their excess energy with this game, which is a little like flag football with a Halloween twist! Have the participants separate into teams, ghosts versus goblins. Prepare "belts" for the players (this can be done in advance, if you know how many you're going to need). Punch a hole in the top of the pictures and put about four of the same picture per belt—enough for each player to have his or her own belt.

When the game starts, the object for your guests is to get as many pictures off the belts of the other team as they can in the designated amount of time—you can choose the time length. When the time is up, the team with the most pictures from the other team wins.

Christmas Games

The holiday spirit is usually in full blast around Christmastime. It's a time to celebrate with friends and loved ones. Playing a Christmas game together will have everyone in a holly jolly mood. So get out the eggnog and cookies, pop in some Christmas jingles, and get ready for these great games that are guaranteed to bring holiday cheer!

Ugly Sweater Competition

When you send out your invitations, you will need to make note of this fun competition. Invite your guests to wear the ugliest Christmas sweaters they can find to the party. When all the guests have arrived, have them gather in a room and vote for the ugliest sweater at the party. The winner can collect a prize, or just be the king/queen wearing the most ugly sweater!

Stuff the Stocking

What You Need

○ Small stockings
○ Small wrapped candies

○ Medium bowl
○ Spoons

Give each guest a stocking and a spoon. Have the candy in the medium bowl in the center of the table. When the game starts, players will have to fill their stocking by the spoonful as fast as they can. The first player to fill the stocking wins the game. Each person can take his or her stocking home as a parting gift or favor.

ALERT

When playing any game that involves candies, it is best to pay attention to the ages of the children at hand. Smaller candies can be choking hazards for some, so softer candies may work better. You can always use a larger stocking if the candies are a bit bigger than could fit in a small stocking.

Oh Christmas Tree, My Christmas Tree

What You Need

○ Green crepe paper
○ Ornament hooks
○ Ornaments, tinsel, garland
○ Timer

Have the participants separate into groups. Each group will need to pick someone to be the Christmas tree. Have all the supplies on a table in the middle of the room and set the timer to three minutes.

When the timer starts, one player from the team will have to go to the table, grab the green crepe paper, and wrap the chosen person up like a Christmas tree. The team members will then go back and forth with each person grabbing only one decoration item and arranging it on the "tree" as quickly and neatly as possible. When the time is up, the host will judge the best tree and the winner receives a prize.

Christmas Carol Charades

What You Need

- ○ Paper
- ○ Pen
- ○ Bowl

All you really need for this game is knowledge of classic Christmas carols. Write down the names of the carols and place them in a bowl. Have your guests gather around and pick a person to start the game. The person will pull the name of a carol out of the bowl and act out the name without saying anything. The person that guesses correctly wins that round and gets to pull the next carol and act it out. The person who guesses the most correct Christmas titles wins the game.

Other Holiday Games

There are well-known holidays that everyone celebrates, and then there are the holidays that are equally fantastic but aren't as well-known. Here are a few games that celebrate these lesser-known holidays—you never know, you might just start a new holiday tradition!

Mardi Gras Bead Thief

What You Need

- ○ Assortment of beaded necklaces

This game involves paying close attention to what you say during the party. As your guests arrive, you will give them each three beaded necklaces. Also, inform them of a few words that they are forbidden from saying while at the party. The words you choose can be Mardi Gras–related or common words that will be hard not to say without really thinking before speaking. If you catch someone saying any of the words, you get to take a pair of beads from that person.

If someone catches you saying one of the words, then that person takes a pair of your beads. The person with the most beads at the end of the night is the king or queen of Mardi Gras.

St. Patrick's Day Dress-Off

What You Need

○ Assortment of green, wearable items (shirts, hats, beads, buttons, wigs, pants, socks)
○ Garbage bag
○ Music

This game can be played and enjoyed by all ages. Start by placing all of the green, wearable items in a bag and set up the music. Have all the guests gather around in a circle, and hand the bag to one of the players.

When the music starts, the players start to pass around the bag. When the music stops, that player closes his or her eyes and reaches into the bag, grabs one item and puts it on. Once the music starts back up, the passing of the bag continues around. This will go on until all the items are emptied. The host of the party can judge the outfits and pick the winner of Saint Patrick's Day.

FACT

St. Patrick's Day has been celebrated for over 1,000 years. It is a celebration of the feast of Saint Patrick, one of the saints to bring Christianity to Ireland, and this marks the day of his death. Most people wear the color green to celebrate Irish heritage and culture.

Fourth of July Tag

What You Need

○ Plastic coins in red, white, and blue (enough for each player to have a coin, with the colors distributed evenly among players)

Gather all of the little patriots around for a crazy game of tag. Give each player one coin of any of the three colors. When the game starts, the mission is to tag people and take their coins. This continues until someone can get three coins, one of each color. When someone loses all three of his or her coins, that person is out and must go sit down. Also, this game is best played outside as to avoid any damage from running. The players can soft tag, but no slapping or hitting of any sort.

QUESTION

Where do you find colored coins?
Party stores, either online or brick-and-mortar, have coins available in red, white, blue, and other colors. If you find yourself needing the coins sooner rather than later, and you can't find them in the right colors, you can always spray-paint regular coins, or round pieces of cardboard, to the colors you need.

Thanksgiving Feast

What You Need

○ Chairs for all but one player

Anyone can join in on this game for a little bit of turkey-day fun. Place all the chairs in a circle and have the guests take a seat, electing one guest to stand in the center of the circle. This person will be the feast caller. Have the caller assign a food (turkey, stuffing, yams, and pumpkin pie) to each of the players, being as even about it as possible.

Depending on the size of the group, you can name as many foods as you like, as long as there are three or more players in each food group. The caller will start the game by calling out one of those food groups. Everyone in that group will stand up and try to find another seat, and the caller scrambles to steal a chair as well. The last person standing has to be the feast caller this time around. This continues as long as you like and as long as fun is still in sight.

CHAPTER 15

Bible and Vacation Bible School Games

In a world of cell phones and social media, it seems like everything is about instant gratification, leaving very little room for connecting one-on-one with other human beings. Attending Bible school is a great way to help keep the youth connected with each other. It's a way to build faith and educate one another about the responsibilities of being in a community. The following games are set to help with the understanding of patience, respect, and faith.

Preschooler Bible Games (Ages 3–5)

Helping a preschool-aged child study the Bible takes real patience. Finding ways to help the little ones to understand and relate doesn't have to be difficult though. If you try creating an atmosphere of playtime while learning, it is sure to get them on the path of faith and biblical understanding. You just have to find the game that works right for you.

The Seed

6 or more players

What You Need

○ Watering can with water

This Bible game is based on the parable of the growing seed, Mark 4:26–29. This game is definitely best if played outside for a little water fun. Have the kids gather around in a circle and sit on the floor.

Choose one person to be the gardener for this game and hand that person the watering can. This person is to walk around the outside of the group and when the person chooses, he or she is to water someone and then take off running, trying not to get tagged. This person must run around the circle while the watered person is chasing him or her, and sit in the watered person's old spot. If the person is caught, he or she remains "It"; if the person sits down in time, then the watering can goes to the person chasing him or her.

David Finds Goliath

What You Need

○ Table
○ Blindfolds

David challenged Goliath, the giant, to a duel when he couldn't stand to hear someone mock the Lord and his people. This game centers on David's defeat of Goliath in the name of the Lord. Start by having the children break into pairs. One child will play David, and the other will be Goliath.

Blindfold both children and have them stand one on each side of the table. The mission is for David to catch Goliath. They must keep one hand on the table at all times while playing. Goliath is trying to avoid being caught by listening for David's approach, and David is trying to catch Goliath by listening for his location. They move around the table until Goliath is caught, and then the next pair will do the same.

The Guide

What You Need

○ Bible
○ Blindfolds

This game helps build trust among the group. If you can create some obstacles in the room, it will make for a more interesting game. Have the children pair up with one another and hand them a blindfold. Have one of the two put the blindfold on, and place the Bible at the other end of the room. Have the pairs stand apart from one another, and the one who is blindfolded will have to listen and be vocally guided by his or her partner across the room to the Bible. The team to safely make it to the Bible first wins. You can explain at the end that they are all really winners because they were guided in the right direction by listening to God's word.

Kids' Bible Games (Ages 6–9)

Kids begin to absorb the Bible once they are able to identify with the issues the Bible presents. Using the following games, you can explain the content of the Bible to the children without going over their heads and leaving them feeling confused.

The Flood

What You Need

- ○ Two buckets
- ○ Marker
- ○ Plastic cups with holes poked in them
- ○ Water

Mark one bucket with a line at the halfway point and fill the other bucket with water. Have the children sit down in a line and place one bucket at each end of the line. The first person will get a cup and fill it with water from one bucket. He or she will then walk it to the other end of the line while holding it over the heads of the other players, dump it into the empty bucket, and then return to his or her seat.

The next child in line will stand up and do the same thing. This will continue until the bucket has been filled to the halfway point. When the kids are done, you can have them ask themselves a couple of questions pertaining to Noah and the flood. Like, "How did it feel to be rained on for so long?" and "How do you think Noah felt when he was asked to build the ark?"

FACT

In the Bible, Mark 4:26–29 (New International Version) says, "This is what the kingdom of God is like. A man scatters seed on the ground. Night and day, whether he sleeps or gets up, the seed sprouts and grows, though he does not know how. All by itself the soil produces grain—first the stalk, then the head, then the full kernel in the head. As soon as the grain is ripe, he puts the sickle to it, because the harvest has come."

Shepherds and Sheep

This is a fun little game of tag with a biblical twist. Have the children split into two teams; one will be the shepherds and one will be the sheep. Have each team stand opposite of one another in the middle of a room. The wall behind each team will act as their safety zone.

To begin the game, call out "shepherds." The shepherd team must run to tag the sheep before they reach their safety zone. You will then switch it up and call out "sheep," and the sheep will then try to tag the shepherds before they reach their safety zone. If they are tagged, they become a part of the opposite team. Play continues until almost everyone is on one team.

Sword of God

What You Need

- ○ Foam swords
- ○ Tape
- ○ Foam balls

Divide the room into two halves by using the tape to mark a line on the floor. Have the children separate into two teams and stand on opposite sides with their swords. Ask the kids to name some sins that they see around them each day.

For each sin throw one of the balls in, going back and forth between sides. Once the sins are listed the children can begin to play the game. The object of the game is to use the sword to battle the sins, and the mission is to knock the balls into the other team's area. The team that has the least amount of balls on their side at the end of the games wins.

Tween Bible Games (Ages 10–12)

Tweens tend to question everything about themselves and about their lives. Questioning their religion is just par for the course. Use these games to help solidify their faith and answer some of their questions.

Biblical Me

Give each guest around twenty minutes to look through a list of Bible characters and choose which person would best match his or her own character. Everyone must then stand up and explain to the rest of the group why that Bible character was chosen as closest to him- or herself.

This game also helps the group understand that everyone has flaws and imperfections, yet everyone is blessed with something unique. Some good biblical figures you can use are Abraham, Noah, Sarah, Jonah, Adam, Eve, Moses, David, Mary, Peter, Paul, and Rebecca.

ALERT

When reviewing Bible characters, younger readers may run across some things that need to be explained. It's best to be prepared in advance to answer questions, as well as to make sure everyone knows that it's okay to ask questions in the first place.

Bible Verse Relay

What You Need

❍ Bible for each group
❍ Paper
❍ Pen

For this game you will need to prepare a list of Bible verses that you would like to cover after the game. Have a list available for each team. Ask the players split into groups and place a Bible beside each group. The mission is for one of the players to read off the verse, then locate it in the Bible and write down the appropriate page number.

The next player will find the next verse and write down the page. This continues until the list is completed. The team to locate the pages from the list the quickest wins the game. Once the game is complete, you can have each person pick a verse he or she would like to discuss.

Teen Bible Games (Ages 13 and Up)

Sometimes it takes a little more than talk to pique the interest of a teen. As teens begin to experience more adult problems, issues will arise that can be answered with biblical defining. The following games and activities should help teens become more engaged in Bible study.

Verse Pop

What You Need

- ○ Latex balloons
- ○ Music
- ○ Slips of paper
- ○ Pen and marker

To prepare for this game, you will need to write down several Bible verses and moral-based questions, and fill in the blank psalm lines on the slips of paper. Take the the psalm line, "The Lord is my _____, I shall not want" for example. Where the blank is, the person guessing would fill in with the correct answer—in this case, the answer is *shepherd*. Put one slip in each balloon, inflate with air, tie off, and number it with a marker. Toss the balloons all around the room before your guests arrive.

When it is time to play the game, have all the participants enter the room, being careful of the balloons. When the music begins, the guests are to pick up the balloons and pass them around to one another until the music stops. The balloon that they are holding when the music stops is now their balloon.

Call out a number. The person with that number on his or her balloon will pop it and read the slip inside. The person will read the slip of paper aloud and answer the question or fill in the blank. That person now gets to call the next number. This continues until everyone's balloon is popped.

FACT

Having a Bible handy during game play can help to eliminate any confusion or embarrassment. The Bible can act as a refresher for players before the games begin. Make sure to use the version of Bible that you prepared the games with as well, in case someone wants to check an answer during the game.

Bible Building

What You Need

- ◯ Poster boards
- ◯ Sticky notes
- ◯ Pens

Before the party begins make a list of important events that occurred in the Bible, making sure not to put them in any type of order. Separate the teens into teams and give each team a poster board, pens, and sticky notes. Post the sheet of biblical events, and each team will have to write down the events, one per sheet, on the sticky notes. They will use the poster board to attach the sticky notes in order of how the events occurred in the Bible. The team to complete this most quickly, with the least amount of mistakes, wins the game.

Group Bible Games

Coming together as a group in the name of worship can be a comforting moment for people, being surrounded by those that feel and believe as they do. Try adding some game-play to your fellowship for some uplifting fun!

Hidden in the Catacombs

For many years, the Romans persecuted Christians for their religious views. The Christians found themselves hiding in the catacombs in order to worship without being found and punished. This game raises the question of what would it be like to have to hide in order to survive. Have all the guests gather around. You all have thirty seconds to hide somewhere. The players will try to find one another, and if you spot someone or someone spots you, you have to stay hidden together. The game ends when there is only one player left not hiding in a group.

FACT

Here are some interesting facts about the Bible that you may not have known. About fifty Bibles are sold every minute, making it the highest-selling book out there. In turn it is also the most shoplifted book on the shelves. There are sixty-six books in the Bible; thirty-nine Old Testament, and twenty-seven New Testament.

Problems and Proverbs

What You Need

- ○ Paper
- ○ Pens
- ○ Bibles

This game is really a great opportunity for people to get to know one another by working together to meet a goal. Have the group break into two smaller groups. Give each team a Bible, pens, and paper. At the start of the game, go around the room and ask the players to name different struggles people commonly face in life. Write them down on the paper.

Once everyone has named a struggle, the groups must now work together to choose a proverb that would apply to each particular struggle. The first team to finish their list wins the game. The teams will take turns reading off each struggle and which proverbs they had chosen to apply to it.

Where, Oh Where

What You Need

- ○ Paper
- ○ Pens (at least two)
- ○ One or more copies of the Bible (optional)

This game will have everyone searching his or her knowledge of the Bible in an attempt to figure out where each biblical person was first mentioned. You will need to make a list of figures (preferably commonly known ones) that appear in the Bible, and keep an answer sheet that notes where each figure is first found. Have your guests separate into two teams. Give each team a pen and a sheet of paper with all of the biblical names listed. Each team has five minutes to list as many locations where the biblical figures first appear as possible. Unless your group is extremely knowledgeable, you might want to provide each team with a copy of the Bible. Here are a few names to get you started.

Book of the Bible	Characters
Genesis	Enoch, Lot, Abel, Noah, Sarah, Jacob, Esau, Rachel, Abraham
Acts	Priscilla, Stephen, Dorcas, Paul, Agrippa, Felix
Judges	Gideon, Deborah
Daniel	Nebuchadnezzar, Abednego, Shadrach, Meshach
Esther	Haman, Esther

Faith-Building Bible Games

The Bible is one of the few books that no matter how many times you read it, you will always notice something new. Faith building is important part of Bible study. Have fun, and help build faith by encouraging one another with biblical playtime and trivia.

Pie à la Fisherman

What You Need

○ Pie tins
○ Whipped cream
○ Gummy fish

Jesus dealt with constant criticism and disbelief from the people he was trying to help. He wasn't afraid of having to fish for the good in men. This game is a symbol of that faith. Put the fish in the bottom of the pie tins and cover them with whipped cream. Prepare one for each player. The players will place their hands behind their back and must fish out each gummy using their mouth, and one by one, put them aside. The person to "fish out" all the gummy fish first wins the game.

QUESTION

What are some activities that a family can do to help build their faith? Have you ever heard the saying, "A family that prays together, stays together"? Taking time to read scripture together, playing a fill-in-the-blank game with psalms and proverbs, and discussing important events in the Bible and how they apply to everyday life are all great ways to increase your faith as a family.

Stones of Faith

What You Need

❍ Stones
❍ Felt squares of different colors
❍ Black marker

To prepare for this game, you will need to write down a section of the Bible that you would like discussed on each piece of felt. Line up the pieces of felt like you would in hopscotch. Hand each player a stone and then line up in front of the felt pieces. The first player will toss the stone, and wherever it lands on the felt is where the person will hop to and name something that he or she knows about that section of the Bible. If the person cannot quote anything, he or she has to sit out. The last person still going wins this game.

CHAPTER 16

Girls-Only Games

Girls love the company of other girls. Whether they want to talk with someone about boys, paint nails, listen to music, or play dress-up, girls love to hang out. Finding the right games to keep them entertained is now easier with the following collection of girl-oriented games and activities. With a few supplies and a little preparation, smiles are sure to follow.

Slumber Party Games

Every girl should experience a slumber party at least once in her life, no matter the age. Getting together with a bunch of girlfriends is good for the soul. So break out the snacks, and get ready for some giggles, because you have one crazy slumber party ahead of you.

Sleeping Cutie

Giggling uncontrollably is just a part of a slumber party, but trying to control the laughter is a different story altogether. Select one child to be the "sleeping cutie" and have her lay flat on her back, arms by her sides. The other participants are to gather around and try everything in their power to make sleeping cutie laugh.

If someone makes sleeping cutie laugh, then that person becomes the sleeping cutie. If the sleeping cutie manages to stay still and not laugh, she gets to pick someone to take her place. This game can continue for as long as you like.

Flashlight Tag

What You Need

○ Flashlights

Though this is usually an outside game, with some adjustments, it can be played indoors. Give each child a flashlight and assign, or take, a volunteer for who would be "It" first. The person who is "It" has to close her eyes and will count to thirty while the others are off hiding. Once she reaches thirty, "It" can use her flashlight to find people. If a player is flashed while hiding, she is out of the game. The last person to get caught is the winner.

If you choose to play a game outside with a group and it is getting dark, it is best to take precautions. Having everyone stay in pairs or in groups when playing the game is a great way to keep everyone accounted for. This will also give a sense of direction and security for those not used to playing in the dark.

Who's There?

When sending out your invitations to the slumber party, ask your guests to bring their sleeping bags. It's sometimes good to have an extra at your house in case someone forgets or doesn't have one.

When you're ready to play the game, have everyone put her sleeping bag on the floor in a circle. Select someone to be "It," and she will leave the room and count to thirty. Everyone in the room is to find a sleeping bag, get inside, and pull it up over her head. "It" comes back into the room, picks a sleeping bag to poke, and asks two questions. The person inside can disguise her voice, but she can't lie when she answers the questions. "It" has to try to guess who is in the bag. If she is correct, the person can come out, and if not, she will move on to the next bag. This continues until someone is figured out.

Tea Party Games

Tea parties can be thrown to help teach manners, to celebrate a birthday, or just to sit down with a cup of tea and converse for a bit. But while you are enjoying your tea and crumpets, if you feel like cutting loose, here are several fun games to help.

Musical Tea Cups

What You Need

○ Teacups
○ Table with chairs

○ Music

Place all but one teacup for each person attending around the table. Have the guests gather around the table as well. When the music begins, everyone will circle the table. When the music stops, everyone must take a seat and grab a teacup. The person without a seat is out of the game. Take away one teacup and chair. The game continues until there is only one person left, and she becomes the Tea Party Princess.

Top Servers

What You Need

○ Two tables
○ Settings for each table (napkins, teacups, saucers, spoons, sugar, linens)

Separate the guests into two teams and assign them an empty table. When the game starts, one person from each team will run to the table and put the linens on and run back. The next person will put one more item on the table and run back. This continues until one of the team's tables is set. The first team to complete the task wins.

FACT

There are a wide variety of teas available for someone hosting a tea party. If you host a sampling session during the party, your guests will have an opportunity to learn about the different types of tea. Green teas, white teas, Earl Grey, Constant Comment, and many others will give you a great selection.

Tea Relay

What You Need

○ Tea
○ Teacups

○ Saucers

For this relay game you will have the group separate into teams. Set a starting line and another point to have the players use as a turn-around point. Fill each teacup up to the top with tea and place each one on its own saucer. The teams are to line up, and the first player of each team should pick up the teacup and walk it to the turn-around point and then go back to the beginning of the line. She will then pass the cup to the next player, and that player will do the same as before. This continues until everyone on the team has had a turn. The team with the most tea left in their cup at the end of the relay is the winner.

Dress-Up Party Games

Dress-up is a great game all by itself. Playing dress-up asks the players to use their imagination, which nurtures their creative side. Let the fantasies fly at your next dress-up party and try out the following variations to give dress-up a new twist.

Nail Break

What You Need

○ Press-on nails
○ Oranges

A game like this will take a bit of skill. Have each girl put on a full set of press-on nails using the adhesive pads. Each girl will receive an orange that she is to peel using her nails. The mission is to peel the orange and try to break the least amount of nails while doing so. The girl who has the most nails on her hand after peeling her orange wins the game.

Fashion Show-Down

What You Need

- ❍ Used clothes, accessories, and jewelry
- ❍ Safety pins
- ❍ Bags
- ❍ Scissors

This is a good activity to get creative juices flowing and to generate a little healthy competition. Have all of the fashion supplies stacked on a table, and hand a bag to each participant. Give the "designers" five minutes to sift through the fashion pieces and put in their bags what they feel they will use.

The players will now have ten minutes to put together a great piece of fashion from what they have chosen. When the time is up, each player tries on her original piece and does a little spin for everyone. The group will then vote for which fashion piece they believe is best.

FACT

Did you know that from the beginning of fashion design, the designers did not use models to show off their pieces to their clients? Instead they would put the designs on dolls and present them to the client for viewing. So in essence, those who play dress-up with their dolls are little fashion designers on their own.

Nail Spin

What You Need

- ❍ Clear-coat polish
- ❍ Several colors of fast-dry nail polish

For this game, have everyone gather around in a circle and place the clear-coat polish on its side. Give each person a different color of finger-nail polish, and have players place their bottles of polish in front of them. Each player will take a turn at spinning the clear-coat bottle in the middle.

Wherever the polish stops and points to is the color that the player has to paint one of her nails. The person who was behind that color of polish will go next. This continues until the first person has all of her nails painted, and that person is the winner!

Spa Party Games

Have a seat, relax, and get pampered; that is what a spa party is all about. Doing hair, facials, and nails will make any girl feel fabulous.

Makeup Madness

What You Need

- ◯ Variety of makeup
- ◯ Makeup applicators
- ◯ Face wash, makeup remover
- ◯ Pieces of fashion for different occasions and styles, like wedding veils, dance tutus, costumes, etc.

Have guests pair up with partners for this one. Have all of the makeup, applicators, and clothing in one spot that can be easily accessed by the players. The pairs will pick pieces of clothing and makeup from what's available and try to dress up the partners to look as if they are attending an event. The partners will then show off their makeup and fashion wear for votes. The pair that has the most votes wins this fashionable game.

FACT

Did you know that there are several different types of spa treatments around the world? In Israel you can get a snake massage treatment; in Turkey, tiny fish nibble at your feet during your pedicure; and in Mexico, you can enjoy a cactus massage. Ouch! You can also indulge in a bird-dropping facial that the geishas in Japan helped develop.

My Spa, Your Spa

What You Need

- ○ Large bowls of warm, soapy water
- ○ Towels
- ○ Nail polish, stickers, glitter
- ○ Lotion

This is a game to both pamper the guests and allow them to do the work. Have them split up into two groups. One group will be the salon owners and the other group will be the customers. The salon owners will be soaking the customers' hands, drying, applying lotion, and painting and designing their nails.

When they are done, the customers become the salon owners and have to do the same that was done for them. The fabulously fresh guests will then vote for whose nail design was the best. The winner gets to take the nail polish home with her.

Spa Day Relay

What You Need

- ○ Robes
- ○ Socks/slippers
- ○ Facial mud
- ○ Towels

You will need to set a start and a finish line for this game. Put all of the supplies at one end of the room. Have your guests split up into two groups and line up at the start line. When the game begins, the first person in each group will run over to the supplies and put on the socks and robe, wrap the towel around her head, and then cover her face in mud. She will then run back to her team and take off the socks, robe, and towel and hand them to the next player in line. This player must put on all the items and run to put the facial mud on. She will then run back to her team and take off the items. When everyone has had a turn, the team that finished first wins the relay.

Princess Party Games

If your little princess wants to have a fairytale-themed party, you definitely want to feature some games that follow suit. This way all the little princesses can burn off some of their energy.

Royal Jewels

What You Need

- ○ Assortment of beads and rhinestones (used for necklace making)
- ○ Several colors of sand
- ○ Jewelry string
- ○ Jewelry clasps
- ○ Several containers

This game is also an activity and a take-home party favor. To prepare you will need to pour a different color of sand in each container. Split up the types of beads and rhinestones and place them in the container and mix them up with the sand. Have the little princesses gather around and decide what kind of jewelry they would like to make. Cut a piece of jewelry string for them and tie a clasp to one end so that the beads will stay on.

When the game starts, the girls will sift through all of the sand, finding all the royal jewels they can in order to make their jewelry. Once they have found their pieces, they can begin making their own royal jewelry. When the girls are done, they can look at each other's pieces and trade if they like.

Kiss on the Frog

What You Need

- ○ Large printout of a frog
- ○ Lipstick or tinted gloss
- ○ Blindfold
- ○ Marker
- ○ Double-sided tape or tacks

Many little princesses dream of finding their prince! Of course, the story sometimes goes that the prince is a frog and only true love's kiss can change him back. This game is the princesses' chance to kiss their prince. Start by hanging the frog on the wall at a height where the girls will be able to see it face-to-face. Each girl will put on some lipstick and the blindfold. They will then try to plant a kiss on the lips of the frog. After each girl has gone, use the marker to note whose kiss it was. After everyone has had her turn at kissing the frog, the person with the closest kiss wins the game.

ALERT

When playing a game that requires children to share lipwear or make-up, you should take precautions because of illnesses and germs. You can have extras of the items, use applicators, or use a butter knife to trim a layer off after each use. That way, everyone is in a sanitary environment.

Pass the Crown

What You Need

○ Plastic crown
○ Candy
○ Princess music

A princess needs a crown to establish that she is indeed a princess, and this game gives each player a chance to win that crown. Have all the royal ladies gather around in a circle. Place the crown on the head of any of the girls and start the music. The players must take the crown and place it on the head of the person next to them. As long as the music is playing, the passing continues.

When the music stops, the person with her hands on the crown has to sit out. She is given a piece of candy and can watch the rest of the game. Once it is down to the last two players, they will pass the crown back and forth between them until the music stops, and the person holding the crown is out. The last person wins the crown and gets to take it home as a prize.

Baking Party Games

Watching your parents cook is a highlight of growing up. It teaches children how to cook for themselves and to learn all the recipes they look forward to eating each week. A baking party is an opportunity to teach the little bakers some awesome recipes and get creative while you bake.

Baker's Delight

What You Need

- ○ Assortment of pastries
- ○ Pen
- ○ Paper
- ○ Plates
- ○ Blindfold

This one helps to take care of part of the snacks for the party. Before the guests arrive, cut up the pastries and place them on plates and number each pastry plate. Make sure to keep a list of the plate numbers and the pastry name for your eyes only. Put the plates where the pastries can't be seen and leave pen and paper for the tasters to write down their guesses on. Each child will take turns putting on the blindfold, and with your help, they will sample each piece and write down what they think it is on their paper. At the end of the tasting, tally up everyone's guesses, and the one with the most correct guesses wins.

QUESTION

What is the best way to get cake-decorating supplies if you are on a budget?
Most decorating supplies can be purchased at a dollar store or you can use items you already have. Graham cracker or cookie crumbs, candies, chocolate chips, and using food-coloring gel to give a better color selection will help with cutting costs on supplies and allow you to have plenty for the decorators to use.

Cupcake Competition

What You Need

- ○ Prebaked cupcakes
- ○ Icing and decorations
- ○ Plastic knives for spreading

○ Sticky notes
○ Pens

A little competition is never a bad thing, especially when it's a sweet competition. Have all of the decorating items out and available for the guests. When they arrive, give them a cupcake and allow them to decorate it however they like. Encourage them to get creative and use as many items or as few items as they please to make their cupcake unique.

After they are done, assign them a number and put their cupcake aside with the others. Once everyone has decorated a cupcake, have players vote on which cupcake is the most unique and tasty looking. The winners get a small prize and everyone gets to eat the cupcakes.

Doughnut on a Line

What You Need

○ Miniature donuts
○ String

This game can be played indoors or outdoors and is great for a good laugh. Run a string from one side of the room to the other. If you're outside, you can use trees to run the line from, and if you are inside, you can run the line from wall to wall. Tie a doughnut, one for each child attending, on its own shorter string. Hang the shorter strings from the main line.

Before the game begins, the players must place their hands behind their backs and line up underneath a doughnut. At the start of the game, the players will eat their doughnut as fast as they can without using their hands. The player who finishes their doughnut first wins the game. If the doughnut breaks off and falls to the floor, that player is out.

Neon Party Games

Neon seems like it would be more of a color scheme rather than a party theme. But it is a party craze that is gaining traction, and finding supplies can be a bit hard to do. When doing a hard-to-find party theme, you have to use other methods to get the theme established, and what better way than to center the games around it?

Glow Dance

What You Need

- ○ Black light
- ○ Glow necklaces and bracelets
- ○ Music

As your guests arrive, give them several glow necklaces and bracelets. They will need to put one around each ankle, one around each wrist, and one around their neck. The music will be the cue to start dancing. They are to dance crazy, moving all of their limbs to create a light show. The music will stop periodically, and everyone must freeze. The person whose lights are still moving is out of the game.

Secret Message

What You Need

- ○ Glow-in-the-dark neon markers or paint with brushes (these can be found at craft stores or online)
- ○ A roll of butcher paper, or large pieces of paper that can be taped or hung up (such as a Post-it easel pad)
- ○ Black light
- ○ Tape

Have all of the players line up, and give each one a large piece of paper. Each player must use the markers or paint to write down something about herself that is slightly embarrassing, or something that she thinks nobody knows about. Gather up the papers and hang them on the wall. Turn on the black light, and read the messages one by one. Have everyone guess who each message is about. The person with the most correct guesses wins the game.

FACT

When using a black light for decorations, there are a couple of things you can use that will reflect the light properly. Bright whites, highlighter pens and markers, fluorescent ink, and petroleum jelly are all good to use under a black light.

Blackout Dodge Ball

What You Need

○ Medium plastic balls
○ Glow-in-the-dark neon paint
○ Black light

Prepare for this game by painting the plastic balls with the glow-in-the-dark paint. Have the guests split into two groups. Line all of the balls up in the center between the two teams, turn out the lights, and turn on the black light. When it's time to start, the teams will run in to get a ball and go back to their starting point. They will now throw the ball at one another, trying to hit people on the other team. If the ball hits a player, that person is out. The team with the most players after ten minutes or so of play is the winner.

CHAPTER 17

Boys-Only Games

When they are young, boys and girls tend to have very different ideas of fun. Instead of painting nails, you might find boys wrestling or playing cops and robbers. The following games are based on some of the most popular boy party themes. Of course, they can be played by any gender, and most can be altered for any theme.

Pirate Party Games

Aargh, Matey! There be a pirate party brewing! The number one goal: find the buried treasure. Get your little pirates together to swab the deck or to see who will have to walk the plank. A pirate adventure has begun!

Swabbing the Deck

What You Need

- ○ Two baseball-size plastic balls
- ○ Mop
- ○ Timer

Gather the pirates around for a game of coordination and control. Start by creating a starting line, an object to have the pirates go around, and a finish line. Using the timer, give a player the mop and put the balls on the ground.

When someone yells "Go," the player, using the mop, will swab the deck (push the balls) down the path, around the obstacle, and back to the starting point without losing the balls. Each player will be timed, and once everyone has gone, the times will be rounded up. The player with the best time is the winner.

FACT

Did you know that pirates used to believe that it was bad luck to have a woman on board their ships, or to whistle because it would bring about storms? Pirates also used to steal their ships because they couldn't afford to buy one of their own!

Cannonball!

What You Need

- ○ Foam balls
- ○ Two cardboard boxes

❍ Tape

Begin this game by using the tape to mark two areas, about six feet apart, with a line of tape on each side. Place a box behind each piece of tape. The boxes act as the ships in this game. If a player is behind the tape, it means he is on board, and if he is in front, it means he has fallen in the water and is out of the game. Split the guests into two teams and assign each one a ship/box. Give several foam balls (cannonballs) to each team.

The object of the game is to get as many cannonballs in the other team's ship as possible. Players can take the cannonballs out of their own ship and toss them back into the other team's ship. They can only have one cannonball at a time. After several minutes of play, call the attack to a halt. The team with the least amount of cannonballs in their ship wins the game.

Walk the Plank

What You Need

❍ Piece of cardboard about 6" wide × 4' long
❍ Blue table cover
❍ Pool noodles
❍ 2 eye patches

This game will test everyone's balancing skills. Lay the blue table cover down to make water under the plank. Place the cardboard plank on top of the table cover. Have each player put on his eye patch; now pick one person to walk the plank and the other to be the pirate. Give both participants a pool noodle and have them stand opposite each other on the plank.

When the game starts, the object is for the pirate to knock the person walking the plank into the water, or for the plank-walker to knock the pirate into the water. They must keep their feet on the plank the entire time they sword fight. The winner switches position and plays the next person. The person who stays on and wins the most battles wins the game.

Superhero Party Games

Is there a damsel in distress, a bully to defeat, or a party that needs saving? Somewhere out there, a tiny hero is just waiting for the moment to use his superpowers! Make this superhero party one to remember using these games.

Superhero Snatch

What You Need

❍ Cape
❍ Black eye masks

This game is about the hero capturing as many bad guys as possible. Set two lines around twenty feet apart and choose one participant to be the hero. The hero will put on the cape and the rest of the group, the bad guys, will wear the masks. Have the bad guys stand behind one line and the hero stand in the middle of the two lines.

Everyone will shout "Up, up, and away!" and all the bad guys will run to the other side. The superhero will tag as many people as he can, and those people will sit out. The players will go back and forth until only one bad guy is left. That person is now the hero, and the game starts over again.

QUESTION

Purchasing licensed superhero party supplies can be expensive. What are some ways to cut costs and still keep with the superhero theme?
With any superhero there should be a color scheme that most identifies with that hero. (Batman is black and yellow, Superman is red and blue, and Iron Man is red and gold.) If you stick with solid-colored supplies and incorporate a couple of things with the actual hero on it, you can cut costs in half and still have a superhero dream party.

Superhero Muscles

What You Need

- ○ Large sweatshirts and sweatpants
- ○ Small, air-filled latex balloons
- ○ Timer

Start this game by separating the heroes into pairs. One person will be the superhero and put the sweatsuit on. The other person will stuff the hero with muscles (balloons). Set the timer for one minute. When the clock starts, the stuffer has to put as many muscles in the hero's suit as possible. Once each team has had a turn, the team with the most muscles wins the game. The game can end with everyone popping the balloons as a little bonus.

Fit to Be Webbed

What You Need

- ○ Silly String

This game is a lot like freeze tag, but with a superhero twist. Give each child a can of Silly String, and have everyone step outside. You can choose two different colors of Silly String and have the kids separate into teams if you like. The object of the game is for the kids to use the Silly String to "web" their opponents so they have to freeze where they stand. If the kids are playing in teams, then a team member can unfreeze/de-web his teammate by tagging him. The last person standing or the team with the most players at the end of the game wins.

Monster Party Games

While some children find monsters to be frightening, others consider monsters to be the coolest things ever. If your little monster enjoys the company of other monsters, then throwing a monster bash is a must. Encourage the guests to embrace their monster side by playing a few of the following games.

Monster Marshmallow Toss

What You Need

- A bag of large marshmallows
- Large monster picture (this can either be a premade cutout, or you can use paint to make one yourself on a piece of board)
- Stiff cardboard rectangle, larger than the monster picture
- Scissors
- Hot glue gun
- Two dowel rods
- Tape

Tape the monster cutout to the cardboard piece, or paint a monster onto the board. Use the scissors to cut out the mouth of the monster, being sure to make it big enough to toss a marshmallow through. Glue one dowel rod on each side of the back of the monster so that it will stand when you put it down.

Have the children stand about five feet from the monster, and give them a handful of large marshmallows, around fifteen. One by one, the children will step up to launch their marshmallows and see how many they can get into the monster's mouth. The player with the most marshmallows to land in the mouth of the monster wins the game.

Make a Monster

What You Need

- ○ Paper cups
- ○ Pipe cleaners, googly eyes, pom poms, crayons
- ○ Glue

Using the paper cup as a building block for your monster, you can color it and use any of the supplies that you have to decorate it. Leave the little monsters to dry while the party continues. Once the glue has dried, bring them all out on display. By a show of hands, have kids vote on who they believe has created the best monster. That person wins the game and gets to take home a prize. This is also great because the guests can take their monsters home as a parting gift.

FACT

Werewolves are real! Well, not completely. Did you know that there was once a man in a circus known as the Wolf Boy? The man's face was covered completely in hair, which is caused by a rare disorder called hypertrichosis, better known as "werewolf syndrome," a genetic disorder that can run in families. This rare condition still exists today, and scientists are still discovering things about it.

Monster Hunter

What You Need

- ○ Printouts of several types of monsters from movies
- ○ Index cards
- ○ Pen
- ○ Tape

Cut out the monsters you have printed and tape each one to its own index card. Write the name of the monster on the back. On another index card, write a small description of a movie that the monster was in. Hang the monster pictures on a board with the name of the monster facing toward the board. Have all of the description index cards spread out on a table.

Each child will pick up an index card and read the description. He will then go over to the board and select which monster the card is describing. If he can name what movie the monster comes from, he will get one point. He gets an extra point if he guesses the name of the monster. The hunter with the most points at the end of the game wins.

Dinosaur Party Games

No matter how long dinosaurs have been extinct, the fantasy and excitement that surrounds them is always fresh. Children just can't seem to get enough of the prehistoric beasts! A party is a great way to feed that frenzy. With a dinosaur theme, you can encourage your little anthropologists to explore, hunt, and dig for dinosaurs to their heart's content.

Dinosaur Egg Hatch

What You Need

○ Polka dot balloons or white balloons
○ Two bed sheets
○ Small candies and prizes

This is a game that can replace a piñata and still be just as entertaining. Before you inflate the balloons with air, you should stick a prize or piece of candy inside of it. Put half of the balloons inside one sheet and the other half in the other sheet. The sheets will act as the nests of dinosaur eggs. Separate the guests into two groups and have them name their team if they would like. When the game starts, the players will grab a dinosaur egg and sit on it to help it hatch (pop it). They get to keep the prizes and candy that are in each balloon. Once all the balloons are popped, the players can have a trade with their treasures.

Ice Age

What You Need

- ○ Plastic cups (one for each guest)
- ○ Mini plastic dinosaurs (small enough to fit into plastic cups, one for each guest)
- ○ Water

This game needs to be prepared the night before, so that everything is set and ready to go. Place one mini dinosaur in each cup, and cover with water. Put the cups in the freezer until you need them the next day at the party.

When your guests are ready to play, get the ice age dinosaurs out of the freezer. Give each player a cup. They now have to melt or break the ice to get the dinosaur out. The first person to get his dinosaur loose is the winner and gets a prize. All of the other players still win because they get to take home their dinosaur from the cup.

FACT

Pterodactyls are often referred to as dinosaurs because they have similarities to other dinosaurs and lived during the same time. They were actually flying reptiles and not flying dinosaurs, as believed by most. This also goes for the plesiosaurs, which were water-based reptiles.

Dino Dig

What You Need

- ○ Little plastic bones
- ○ Mini dinosaurs
- ○ Mini shovels
- ○ Paintbrushes
- ○ Candy
- ○ Sandbox with sand

To prepare for this awesome dino dig, you will need to bury the bones and the mini dinosaurs throughout the sand. When your guests are ready to dig for bones, give each one a little shovel and a paintbrush.

As the game starts, players will search the sand for bones and dinosaurs. Each bone is worth one piece of candy and each miniature dinosaur is worth two pieces of candy. As they pull the bones out, tell your guests to use their brushes to clean them off and observe them. As a bonus, if they can name the dinosaur they find, they get another piece of candy.

Military Party Games

Calling all soldiers, calling all soldiers! Get out the camouflage, canteens, and fatigues—it's time for a military party! With the right gear and the right games, you'll have a military party every troop will remember.

No Man Left Behind

What You Need

○ Bed sheet
○ Toilet paper (2 rolls, one for each team)

Split the guests into two teams. Have each group elect two people to be the injured soldiers, who must lie down on the ground at one end of the room. The rest of the team is to go to the other side and get ready to rescue their fellow soldiers. When the game starts, the soldiers grab the toilet paper and run to their fallen teammates. They must wrap one of their injured soldiers in toilet paper and then roll him onto the sheet. As a team effort, they must pull the soldier to safety on the other side of the room (you may want to set a boundary or rules for what is the "safe zone"). They will then run back and do the same thing for the other soldier. The first team to finish rescuing both soldiers wins the game.

Prisoners of War

What You Need

- ❍ Little army men
- ❍ Paint
- ❍ Scissors
- ❍ Poster board

The enemy has captured the men in your unit and it's now up to you and the rest of the unit to save the prisoners of war! Start by choosing two colors that will represent the teams. Divide the army men into two groups. Paint the bottom half of one group with one team color; paint the other group with the other team color. Cut out two flag shapes from the poster board and paint each one the color of a team. Split the guests into two teams and have them name their teams. Hang the flags of the teams somewhere kind of hard to reach, but not impossible. Hide the little army men on the opposite team's side.

Inform each team that they have soldiers that are being held and need to be rescued. Give them the number of soldiers they must collect. Once they have gathered all of the army men, they have to capture the other team's flag. The first team to complete these tasks wins the game. The opposite team can try to deter you by standing in your way or trying to confuse you when you get the flag, but they cannot stop you from getting the army men.

ALERT

Always make sure that when your guests play games that require a lot of running and physical activity that they stretch first so as to avoid any injury. Also make sure to clear the play areas of any debris or potentially dangerous objects so that play can go on safely and uninterrupted.

Rucksack Race

What You Need

- Backpack
- Items for packing (towel, canteen, compass, Band-Aids, food)
- Timer or watch to keep time

It's now time for the soldiers to pack up for a march. The players will be timed to see how fast they can pack up their sacks and then march across the yard and back. Mark off a starting line. Put the items that will go into the backpack on the ground, about ten feet away. When the clock starts, the first player must grab the backpack, run to the supplies, and put the items in one by one.

However, each player must roll the towel, shut the canteen, and put the Band-Aids in a baggy before stuffing them in the sack. Once everything is in the backpack, the player must put it on, march back to the starting line and back, and then unload the sack. When that player comes back to the starting line, the timing stops. Record each player's time. The next player does the same thing, etc., and the player with the best time is the winner.

Totally Gross Games

Children loved to be shocked and surprised. Plus grossing someone out is always good for a laugh. Slime, goo, and sticky stuff make one awesome party theme . . . if you like that sort of thing.

Lots of Crickets

What You Need

- Crickets
- Medium box
- Rubber mice and snakes

Using rubber bugs is a great way to gross people out, but real bugs are even better! Keep in mind that crickets tend to scare people because they jump, so use that to your advantage with this gross game. Place all of the rubber mice and snakes spread out in the bottom of the box or aquarium. Pour the crickets into the box and close the lid so that they do not escape. Have the guests take turns trying to reach into the box and get as many frogs and snakes as they can before thirty seconds is up. The person who gathers the most wins the game.

FACT

When you find yourself in possession of a mess of crickets after a gross game, what should you do with them? Your best solution is to have the children take them outside and release them into the wild once the party has concluded for the evening.

Give a Dog a Bone

What You Need

- ○ Dog bones
- ○ Dog bowls

For this gross little game, you will need to set two dog bowls across the yard or room from each other. Put a pile of dog bones in between the two dog bowls. Split your daring guests up into two teams, and if they like, the teams can choose cool names for the challenge. Have one person from each team start in the center on all fours, with the players facing one another.

When the game begins, they will need to pick up a dog bone with their mouth and crawl to the bowl behind them (their team bowl) and dump the biscuit in the bowl. Then they have to crawl back to the center, stand up, and tag a teammate.

The teammate will then move to the center and get on all fours to repeat the same as the first player. This will continue until all of the bones are gone from the center. If someone drops a bone, he can only pick it up with his mouth. The team that gathers the most bones in their bowl wins the game.

FACT

If you have trouble locating a large quantity of slime in your local stores, you can always make a homemade version. All you need to do is combine the following ingredients in a bowl and let it set: four cups of water, a tablespoon of green food-coloring, and ten cups of cornstarch.

Slimed

What You Need

- ○ Slime
- ○ Two buckets
- ○ Two large bowls
- ○ Aprons

This game can get very messy, so you may want to play this one outside. Fill each bucket half way with slime. Split the guests into two teams and give each team aprons to put on to avoid their clothes getting damaged. Put the buckets on opposite sides of the room and put the bowls side-by-side in the center of the room. Make sure to mark or position bowls so that the teams are aware of which bowl is theirs to fill.

One by one, the teammates will run to the bucket and scoop up slime with their hands and transfer it to the team bowl. You can set a time limit for this game or play until the slime buckets are empty. The team with the most slime at the end of the game is the winner.

Sports Games

Sports are a great way to teach children about participation and teamwork. It's also a means of boosting confidence and incorporating exercise. So, if your little sports fanatic wants to celebrate with his favorite sport, you will need a few games to get the party started.

Where does the game of football come from?
Football is thought to have originated from a game commonly played in ancient Greece. The game was known as Harpaston. There were no real rules for the game other than the mission of getting the ball across a goal line by any means necessary. The game was known for rough tackles and having no limit to the amount of players allowed to participate at once.

Hoops Through Loops

What You Need

○ Hula-Hoop
○ Football

This game is best if played outside in an open area. Prepare for this game by hanging the Hula-Hoop by a tree branch or clothesline. Have the first player line up about five feet from the Hula-Hoop and hand him a football. He will then try to throw the ball through the hoop. If he misses, it will be the next guest's turn. If he makes it through the Hula-Hoop, he must then take a step back and throw again. The person who makes the most successful throws through the hoop is the winner of this game.

Balancing Act

What You Need

○ Golf balls
○ Tennis rackets

For this game you will need to set a start line and a finish line for the players. Give each player a racket and three golf balls. The object of this game is to balance the three balls on the tennis racket and walk from the start line to the finish line as fast as possible without any balls falling off of the racket. If someone drops a ball, he or she must keep going and cannot pick it up.

If no one crosses the finish line with all three balls, the one who crosses over the finish line first with two balls wins the game. You can also have the players with two balls race again to see if they can cross with the three balls still on their rackets.

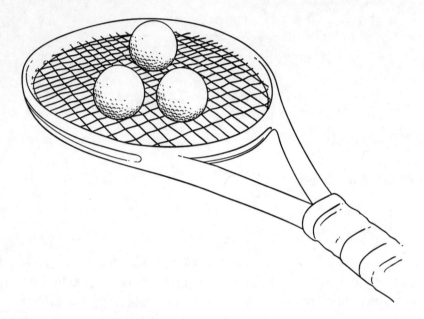

Human Bowling

What You Need

○ 2-liter bottles

This can be a dizzying game, but it's a fun one! Line up a bunch of two-liter bottles on one side of the yard. Have the guests split up into pairs. One player will be the bowling ball and the other player will be the bowler. The ball player will have to do somersaults across the yard, acting like a bowling ball. The bowler will guide the dizzy bowling ball across the yard by shouting directions for the person to reach the bottles and knock them down.

Once the player has rolled to the bottles, that person will try to use his or her body in one last roll to knock down as many as possible. The pairs with the highest scores move on to the next round until there is a winning pair.

CHAPTER 18

Icebreaker Games

At most gatherings, whether it's a party, study group, or the beginning of a new job, you will most likely have that awkward moment when you realize you don't know anyone around you. Getting people to freely talk to one another can be quite the challenge. A good icebreaker game can always get the attendees to relax and laugh a little. You never know—it could put you on the road to making new, lifelong friends.

Games for Getting to Know One Another

Are there a few unfamiliar faces in the room? Do you feel a bit uncomfortable when you are around those you do not know? Break the silence and awkward moments with some entertaining games.

Who Did That?

What You Need

○ Pens
○ Paper

As the players arrive, give each one a pen and a piece of paper. Tell them to anonymously write down the worst job they ever had and one memory they have from that job. They are then to fold up the paper and place it in the bowl. Once everyone has written down his or her worst job, the host will bring the bowl to the front and pick out one piece of paper. The host will read the job and the description, and everyone in the room will try to guess who wrote the description.

For each one that someone guesses correctly, a point is awarded. The person with the most points at the end wins the game. This game is good for introducing people, because they will all have a chance to laugh a little while reminiscing over old job horror stories.

ALERT

Anytime you're playing an icebreaker game in a working environment, it's best to go over company policies beforehand. Every company is different, so going over the policies will save everyone from any potential problems regarding human resources or company leaders. You can usually refer to an employee handbook, or request information from your human resources department.

Webs

What You Need

❍ Yarn or string

With this icebreaker, you can have all the players stand together. Give one person the ball of yarn and have him or her say something personal about him- or herself. The person will then ask the group if there is anyone who can relate to the story and pass the yarn to that person while keeping the start of the string in his or her hand. The next person will relate the last story to a personal story and ask the group if anyone can relate. That person will then pass the yarn to the person who can relate, while keeping a piece of the yarn in his or her hand.

At the end of this game, the person with the first string will pull it, and everyone's hands should move with each tug. This web that has been created will show how everyone has something in common and can relate to one another.

An Interview

Sometimes the best way to get to know someone is to ask questions. With this game, the players will be conducting interviews with a random person. Participants will pair up with someone in the room that they do not know and ask that person ten different questions. Depending on the environment, you may want to prepare and approve your questions, or you could let the players shoot from the hip. Once they have all their answers, participants will go around the room and introduce their partner and announce the things that they learned about the person. This way everyone in the room gets to know the person being introduced as well.

Games to Set the Mood for Laughter

Having a few giggles can lighten the mood for any group. Here are some ideas for getting everyone laughing without putting anyone on the spot.

Whose Shoe?

Creating an environment that is rich in laughter can be challenging, especially if it's in a room filled with people who aren't familiar with one another. For this game you will take your group and ask them all to remove either their left shoe or right shoe and place them in a pile in the middle of the room. When the game starts, players grab a random shoe and put it on, whether it fits or not. They will then have to find the person wearing the other shoe and introduce themselves.

Face-to-Face

The funny factor in this game will depend on what the players choose to say. To play this game, the first player will start things off by saying a number and a body part. For example, if that person were to say "three knees," then three people would need to put their knees together. The next person will name a number and a body part, and the group will work together to fulfill the request. Once the players begin running out of parts, the game can wind down with crazy requests like ten noses. It's impossible to complete yet still funny to think about.

FACT

Laughter has always been seen as some of the best medicine. It's a simple and inexpensive way to lift spirits in a bad time. You can always get a crowd going if you have a quick game of laughs: Have people do their goofiest laugh out loud, and enjoy a genuine laugh in the process.

Opposites

For this game, have everyone stand in the middle of the room. Begin by saying something like, "After I get dressed in the morning, I brush my teeth before I eat." Everyone that does this will go to one side of the room. The people who don't do this go to the other side. The players will then introduce themselves to the person to the left of them.

The next person will shout out another random thing about him- or herself. People in the group will again go to the side of the room based on what they do and introduce themselves to the person to the right of them. This continues until everyone has named something random.

Games to Help Everyone Relax

Everyone gets stressed-out now and again. Attending a party should help relieve these stressors. Get-togethers are the perfect setting for relaxing and forgetting all your worries. Try a few of these games to help everyone relax at your next party.

Deserted

The premise for this game is simple, but it is an excellent way to get everyone talking. Ask your guests to pretend they are going to be left on a deserted island soon. They must pick three partygoers to bring with them. The players now go around talking to one another, finding out each other's qualities and abilities. This will, in turn, help the players make a decision about who they would choose to bring to the desert island with them. Have everyone announce who he or she picked, and why.

Sculpturenary

What You Need

- ❍ Clay or Play-Doh
- ❍ Plastic knives for cutting
- ❍ Scraps of paper
- ❍ Pen

Write down several different animals, foods, and activities on the scraps of paper. Fold the papers up and put them in a bowl. Have the players take turns pulling a piece of paper and reading what's written to him- or herself. Everyone will get two minutes to use the clay to build whatever was written on the paper. Others will try to guess what it is that they are trying to make. The person who guesses correctly gets to go next. The person with the most correct guesses wins the game.

FACT

A great way to relieve stress and relax a little bit is to use a stress ball. While these can be purchased inexpensively, there is also an easy way to make a stress ball at home. Fill a latex balloon with half a cup of cornstarch and half a cup of flour and tie shut. You'll find yourself playing with these and relaxing quite easy.

Going to the Moon

To finish this game, your guests will need to pay attention and use their creativity. The game will start off by having everyone gather around at a table. The first person will start this icebreaker by saying, "I (name) am going to the moon and I am taking (item) with me." The next person will then have to say, "I (name) am going to the moon and I am taking (first person's name)'s (item name) and (his or her chosen item)." This will continue for as long as everyone can remember people's names and what their items are. The last two people are the winners of this game.

M&Ms and Me

What You Need

○ M&M candies

Before starting the game, you will need to assign a subject to the colors in the bag of candies. For example, blue could be family, red could be hobbies, and green could be cars. As your guests arrive, give each one a handful of candies and inform them of the color-coding. Have the guests go around and ask one another questions based on what color of candies they have. By the end of the night, guests will have to talk about what they learned about each person in the room.

Games to Incorporate Trust

Trust is a very difficult thing to establish, especially between strangers. Here are a few games that will help build trust between new or old friends.

Sitting Together

Have everyone in the group stand in a circle and turn to the left or right; everyone must turn in the same direction. They will then need to move close to one another, almost touching. When the leader says "Go," participants will slowly take a seat, and should land on the knees of the person behind them. It will look as though the entire group is sitting down. Now they will have to trust one another to support each other's weight and to move as one when the leader says to. As long as the team can stay together, the leader can keep the game going.

Life Happening

What You Need

○ Pen
○ Paper

Before your guests arrive, write down several everyday scenarios on scraps of paper, and put them into a bowl. When the gathering begins, have everyone split into small groups. The first person to go in each group will pull out a paper and read it silently. That person must then act out the scenario, but without using any words at all. Players can make gestures and light noises, but no words of any kind. The team with the most correct guesses in a set amount of time (say, fifteen minutes) wins this game.

A common activity that employers and therapists use to help people build trust with one another is called "The Fall." "The Fall" is when you have a person stand behind you and you drop backward, trusting that the person is going to catch you. If you are in need of something to help create trust but have very little time, you should give this activity a shot.

Tangled Up!

This game requires the team to work together to fix a problem they are presented with. The problem in this case is a big tangled mess. Have the group begin the game by interlocking themselves with one another. They can lock arms, legs, go through each other's legs—anything goes as long as it is in keeping with trying to create a knot. Once everyone is tangled up, have one person give commands on how to undo the web of people.

Icebreakers for Small Groups

Sometimes it takes certain people longer than others to warm up to strangers—and that's okay! If this is the case for you or any of your friends, you might want to try a game to break the ice.

Honey, I

This game is great for smaller groups. Have one person volunteer to go first or assign someone. This person will walk up to a random person and say, "Honey, I love you," and that person will respond with, "Honey, I love you, but I can't laugh." The person who started cannot laugh or do whatever it is that the other person named. If the person does it accidentally, he or she is out of the game. Otherwise, he or she can move on to the next person.

QUESTION

What are some simple, tasty, and inexpensive foods that can be served to a small group of people?
Anytime you are planning to have a small group over, or if you are going to be involved in a small group, you want to go easy on the food. In most situations you don't have time for a full meal, so snacks and finger foods work wonderfully. Foods like mini sandwiches, chips, pickles, veggies, fruits, and crackers with cheese are ideal.

Sentence Roundup

What You Need

- Chalkboard/dry erase board
- Chalk/markers

Have the group break up into two smaller groups for this game. The first person in each group will need to grab a piece of chalk or dry erase marker and write down one word to start a sentence. The next person in the group will go up and write down one word. This will continue until the group has written a sentence together as a team. Sometimes this game can be quite funny when it comes time to read the sentence. This game helps the group to focus on anticipation and working together toward a common goal.

Personality Hunt

Start the game by giving the people in the room a list of things they will need to find that relates to their personality. Items can be something that they adore, someone that is extremely close to them, a wonderful memory they have, and what they ate for breakfast. The items can be random or have a close link to the thing they're thinking of. The players can search their purses, pockets, and the general area for items that will remind them of each statement. When they are done, they will all share with the group.

Icebreakers for Large Groups

Large groups are very easy to get lost in. Whether you want to blend in or to stand out, it is necessary to at least get familiar with the people that surround you. Communicating in a large group can be complicated because of noise level or cliques. Jump into icebreaking in a large group with these activities and games.

Big Circle, Little Circle

Have your group split into two even teams. One team forms a circle facing outward. The other team will get in a circle around them, facing inward. The teams should be face-to-face with one another. They will begin by saying something they enjoy about, or have in common with, the person they are face-to-face with. The circle will then shift one step to the right and the people will continue to ask and answer questions. Everyone should go around the circle at least once before ending the game.

Hats Off

What You Need

- Newspaper
- Glue
- Glitter, feathers, markers

As the players arrive, invite them to create their very own masterpiece fashion hat. They can use any of the supplies available. Once they are done making their hats, participants will do a miniature fashion show to show off their piece to everyone in the room. Later everyone will vote on whose hat was the most creative, and that person wins a prize.

ALERT

Always make sure when you are hosting an event with a large group that you pay close attention to the guests and their whereabouts. You want to make sure that your guests are having a good time and learning about one another and not staggering off by themselves. This is why icebreaker games are important tools to get everyone acquainted.

When I Grow Up . . .

Most people dream of being astronauts, fire fighters, cops, and soldiers when they are children. In this game, gather people together and, one by one, have them say what it is that they wanted to be as a child. They will then reveal what it is that they currently do and if they still aspire to become what they thought they would be.

Once everyone in the group has gone, the host can do a quick game of trivia by going back through and naming the people, then having the group recall what those people wanted to be when they got older. The person with the most correct guesses wins.

Icebreakers for Shy Children

Shy doesn't mean boring. Some of the shyest people are the most fascinating, because they take the time to observe their surroundings. If there are some shy children in your group, you can bring them out of their box and pick their brain with a couple of great games.

Partner Up

What You Need

○ Pens
○ Paper scraps

Before your guests arrive, jot down several different sets of partners from cartoons or children's movies, for example, Mickey and Minnie Mouse,

Batman and Robin, Peter Pan and Tinkerbell, or Dora and Boots. Write down one name from each partnership on a piece of scrap paper.

When the kids arrive at the party, give them a name and tell them to keep it to themselves. Everyone will now go around the party, asking others questions about who they are, what they do, where they live, and so on, in an effort to find their matching character. The person being questioned must answer as if he is the character on his scrap of paper. The first set of partners to find each other wins the game.

Moon Ball

What You Need

○ Building blocks
○ Beach ball

This is a two-part game that will have even the shyest child participating and enjoying him- or herself. Have the children start off the first half of the game by building a small city in the middle of the floor with their blocks. Once the city is complete, the players toss the beach ball—the moon—into the air and keep it in the air. They will be doing this near their city, so while they concentrate on not dropping the moon, they also will need to make sure not to crash their city. If the team can make it without crashing the city or dropping the moon, give them a reward for all of their hard work.

Barnyard Bonanza

What You Need

○ Pen
○ Paper scraps

Before this game starts, write down the names of at least six different animals, one on each piece of scrap paper. Fold up the papers, and as the children arrive, give them a piece of the paper and tell them to read the name of the animal to themselves. They must not tell anyone what animal they are.

The guests will then go around the room making the animal noises, trying to find the other animals like them. As they find one another, they will stick together. The animals to find one another the quickest are the winners of this game.

FACT

Studies show that shy people tend to be better listeners, deep thinkers, rather cautious, and have a welcoming vibe about them. Being shy is often thought of as a handicap, but when given the opportunity to overcome their shyness, children bloom and become social butterflies thirsting for a way to reach out and communicate with others.

Tongue-Tied

What You Need

❍ Plastic cups
❍ Little favors and candies

Begin this icebreaker by filling the cups with about ten pieces of candy and favors. Give each party guest a cup. The object of this game is to catch the other guests saying key words. The key words can be anything you choose, common lingo or slang, or simple words like "fun," "yesterday," "crazy," and "school."

Let the players know what the keywords are before the game begins. If they hear someone else say one of the keywords, they can take an item from that person's cup and put it in their own. This game can go on for a half hour or it can go throughout the party. All the guests will get to know one another with this game. Also, the guests get to keep their cups at the end of the game, so essentially everyone is a winner.

Additional Resources

Magazines

Highlights for Children

This magazine has games, puzzles, and articles that children can enjoy and parents will approve of. There are three different magazines available based on the ages of the audience, which makes it easier for parents to select the right magazine.

Games

This magazine features a variety of puzzles, brainteasers, and trivia quizzes. They also publish reviews of both electronic and nonelectronic games, to help consumers decide which games best suit them (and their children).

Websites

www.pinterest.com

This website is perfect for the do-it-yourself type of party planner. Pinterest supplies a large collection of ideas on parties, games, crafts, and just about anything you could want to include in your next get-together.

www.partygamesplus.com

Games, games, and more games should be the motto for this website. The games listed on this site are organized by not only age but by theme, making it easy for you to select the perfect game.

www.spoonful.com

For a great selection of activities, games, food ideas, and crafts for any party or gathering, this is definitely a choice website.

Quick Games

The following lists highlights some popular games you can buy to play at your next party or family game night. They're easy to find at your local toy store or on Amazon.com.

Spot It!

This game is great for children, easy to learn, and can be played nearly anywhere. Its instructions are easy to follow, and it is played like a memory game and matching game combined.

Hedbanz

This is an awesomely entertaining family game. Each player places a headband on his or her head with a card in it, facing out (you cannot see you own card). Players take turns trying to guess what their card says before the clock is up.

Qwirkle

This game is suitable for children aged six all the way up to older adults. It requires the use of strategy, matching, and some basic math skills. Not only are you playing a great game, you are learning as well.

Wits & Wagers

Wits & Wagers is definitely a top party game. Not only do you have to answer trivia questions, you get to wager, too. It's suitable for groups of three or more.

Would You Rather . . . ?

This game is a series of questions about situations one could be placed in. It is up to your group to decide what choice should be made before time is up. While you're deciding, the other group is debating what move your team will make. This is a game of endless fun.

Index